KT-555-831

PRINCIPLES OF TEACHING APPLIED TO PITMAN'S SHORTHAND

PRINCIPLES OF TEACHING APPLIED TO PITMAN'S SHORTHAND

BY

ROBERT W. HOLLAND

O.B.E., M.A., M.SC., LL.D.

FIFTH EDITION

BY

B. W. CANNING, B.A., P.C.T.

LONDON

SIR ISAAC PITMAN & SONS LTD.

Fifth Edition 1963
Reprinted 1967

SIR ISAAC PITMAN & SONS LTD.
PITMAN HOUSE, PARKER STREET, KINGSWAY, LONDON, W.C.2
THE PITMAN PRESS, BATH
PITMAN HOUSE, BOUVERIE STREET, CARLTON, MELBOURNE
20–25 BECKETT'S BUILDINGS, PRESIDENT STREET, JOHANNESBURG

ASSOCIATED COMPANIES
PITMAN MEDICAL PUBLISHING COMPANY LTD.
46 CHARLOTTE STREET, LONDON, W.1
PITMAN PUBLISHING CORPORATION
20 EAST 46TH STREET, NEW YORK, N.Y. 10017
SIR ISAAC PITMAN & SONS (CANADA) LTD.
(INCORPORATING THE COMMERCIAL TEXT BOOK COMPANY)
PITMAN HOUSE, 381–383 CHURCH STREET, TORONTO

MADE IN GREAT BRITAIN AT THE PITMAN PRESS, BATH
F7—(S.238)

PREFACE

This book has for more than thirty years been a standard work for all those training to become teachers of the office arts.

The qualities of thoughtful, succinct statement, helpful illustration, and wide-ranging subject matter are characteristic of its author, Dr. R. W. Holland, one of the most eminent educationists of this century. The present writer is himself indebted to it for his own first steps in this field of education.

The revision of a work so well esteemed is not lightly to be undertaken. The writer has tried to preserve the known qualities of the book, while introducing those modifications and expansions that the passage of time has made essential.

These revisions will be found to be of three kinds—

1. Alterations bringing references, allusions, and illustrations up to date.

2. Additions or amplifications made necessary by advances in pedagogy and educational psychology.

3. Alterations made advisable by the changed emphasis of the questions asked in the examinations of the Royal Society of Arts Teacher's Certificates and Joint Examining Board's Diplomas, towards which the book is particularly directed.

What Dr. R. W. Holland wrote in his original Preface thirty-seven years ago, remains equally applicable today—

"The author trusts that it will be the means of suggesting to teachers of shorthand the desirability of, and indeed the necessity for, further inquiry into the theories of teaching."

CONTENTS

CHAPTER 1

INTRODUCTORY

The English educational system in its complexity was not originally based on any particular preconceived plan, and first attempts to build a consistent whole are found in the Education Act, 1944. This Act provides a framework for the country's educational system.

For the purpose of this book it is not essential to enter into an analysis of the Act save where it deals with the educational provision that must be made for the individual from the nursery to adult years. To cover all stages of the progressive life of the individual, the Act divides education into three stages, namely, primary, secondary and further education.

Primary Education

All forms of pre-secondary education are nowadays included in the term "primary." Every child must have some form of primary education from the age of five, whilst local education authorities may make arrangements for children who have attained the age of two years, but not yet attained the age of five years, to attend at a nursery school.

Primary education continues until the child is eleven years of age, when the second stage begins. Under former regulations it was the duty of every parent to see that his child received a sufficient education in reading, writing and arithmetic. This, however, in specific terms, has now gone and it is the duty of a parent to see that his child is educated according to his age, aptitude and ability, and it is the duty of the state, through the local authority, to provide facilities for this purpose.

Secondary Education

Secondary education starts at the age of eleven and may continue to the age of eighteen or nineteen years. There is, however, no compulsion beyond the age of fifteen years, but this compulsory limit may at any time be raised to sixteen. Secondary education is to be provided by the local education authority to meet the requirements of individual pupils. It is, of course, impossible to place every child in an educational environment suiting his own particular age, aptitude and ability, but the whole of the school-age population can be broadly divided into three or four categories, and this is done by having three or four types of secondary schools. The first type is by no means new, and coincides with what was formerly known as the "Grammar School" or "High School." It provides for an education based on the mathematical or classical tradition and naturally offers facilities for those whose aptitudes are in this direction. It is difficult to say that ability can be accurately measured at the early age of eleven, as not all children develop at the same rate. Nevertheless, the broad division which produces the grammar-school pupil appears to be a satisfactory one. Pupils whose aptitudes lie in other directions are catered for in either the secondary modern school or the secondary technical school, which latter includes the secondary commercial school. There are not very many secondary technical schools, and still fewer secondary commercial schools.

The secondary modern school offers much the same kind of training between the ages of eleven and thirteen as does the grammar school, but in the last two years special subjects take the place of the classics, formal mathematics and the like. The choice of subjects is a wide one not usually directed to any particular vocation, but in many urban centres shorthand and typewriting have been introduced, although it would appear that subjects of a vocational nature were not envisaged as a part of the curriculum. The secondary technical school receives in theory those persons who have specific mechanical and practical group factors of intelligence. In theory these various types of secondary schools are looked upon as equal in status, but it is difficult to break away from the old tradition that the grammar school is superior as a place of education to any other form of secondary school.

Since the segregation of pupils into different kinds of secondary schools raises very important social, as well as educational issues, some important authorities are building up a different organization. They are trying to broaden the scope of the kinds of secondary education provided and at the same time to bring all pupils of secondary age in one area together into one school. These schools, necessarily large, are known as comprehensive schools. A further variation is the "campus" scheme, in which study is carried on in separate schools, but in all else the schools share amenities and mingle freely.

Further Education

The third stage of education provided by the Education Act is known as "further education." Technically this term applies to education provided for all those over compulsory school attendance age, but such provision as is made for those who remain at the secondary school after the age of fifteen years would not, in spite of the wording of the Act, be included in the term "further education" in the sense referred to in the Act. We can take it, therefore, that further education is a provision for those who leave the secondary schools at fifteen or any later age.

Further education is either full-time or part-time education in a normal educational establishment, or leisure-time occupation in such organized cultural training and recreative activities as are suited to the individual's requirements. The latter branch of further education will be offered in county colleges which it was proposed to set up under the Education Act. Some such colleges are already in existence under the title of the "College of Further Education," and they bear a distinct imprint of the organization previously known in small urban areas as the "Technical Institute." All local authorities also make substantial provision these days for adult education, usually from the recreative rather than the vocational viewpoint.

Shorthand in Day Schools

Although shorthand may be readily shown to be of great value in terms of general education, it is generally regarded as a vocational subject. Only in the later stages of secondary education does it find a place in the curriculum. In recent years, the strong influence of office skills in providing motivation for the last year or two of secondary education has been increasingly conceded by educationists. Shorthand may be found in the grammar school which provides a so-called "Commercial Sixth," meaning a form which offers an intensive training in the office arts to those pupils who, having completed the General Certificate of Education in a body of subjects common to the school curriculum, are not prepared to proceed further with their general education. In the opinion of some educational experts such classes are out of place, and would best be provided at the local school of commerce or the technical college. It might be said that the distance to be travelled where such a school is in a rural area is a hardship, but unless the products of the commercial sixth can be absorbed locally the argument is not convincing.

In the curriculum of many secondary technical, secondary modern, and comprehensive schools, shorthand and typewriting are included. These subjects are also to be found in the curriculum of part-time students released from employment, and in many special commercial, shorthand-typist, and secretarial courses organized by technical colleges and colleges of commerce (for young people between the ages of fifteen and eighteen years). A rising number of employers give time and money for the training in commercial subjects of their young employees, though the proportion so released is far less in office work than in technical and scientific employment.

Apart from the foregoing provision in the day-time, much of shorthand and typewriting training is carried out in evening classes, and it is here that the would-be teacher generally obtains his or her first experience of teaching commercial subjects.

We now consider the place of shorthand in our teaching arrangements and also the nature of this education for which we make provision in our various schools.

Education and Teaching

The conclusions that the organizer and inspector of school work draws from his experience must often lead him to doubt whether there is truly a science of education, and he may almost be persuaded that there are no *principles* underlying the art of teaching. This may seem particularly true in the sphere of commercial education.

In an attempt to set out a few ideas on teaching, it is impossible to undertake the task of proving that such a view is wrong, so one is content to affirm that there is a body of fundamental principles to which the practice of teaching can and should conform.

The teacher of commercial subjects, like his fellows in a more general scheme of education, ought to consider the matter for himself in the works of some of the modern writers on the science of education and the art of teaching.

The present work is concerned with the elementary principles of teaching, illustrated by suggestions for the teaching of Pitman's shorthand, and it is first desirable to try to show what is meant by "education" and to show briefly in what manner shorthand can be said to take a place in a scheme of education.

What is Education?

There have been so many definitions of education, some unpractical, some ideal, and many indefinite, that it is well to avoid the direct issue and to give what it may be allowed is a practical definition of an educated person. An educated man is one whose experiences in life have been so provided and organized that he is enabled to serve himself and his fellow-citizens to his fullest capacity. The person whose experiences are so directed that he becomes a "useful citizen" in the best sense of the term is truly educated, for "useful citizen" implies honesty and truth as a man, and both of these, together with skill, as a worker.

It has never been denied that reading, writing, and arithmetic, the formal studies of the primary school, have their places in a scheme of education as the mechanics of general education, "the tools for handling experience." Without reading, the most potent educational influence at hand, the study of good literature, would be lost; yet we realize that reading in itself, even in the early stages, should be subordinated to the subject-matter read.

Shorthand as a Subject

Just as the "three R's" are among the tools through which education may be won, so in the sphere of commerce the study of shorthand and other formal subjects is equally important, always provided that they are kept in proper perspective. Just as writing is not an end in itself, so is shorthand only a means to an end. Immediately it becomes an obsession and occupies too important a place in the eyes of the exponent, it loses its educational value, and comes to rank with the pen exercises and flourishes popular with the writing master of fifty years ago: they were neither art nor handwriting. Shorthand is an invaluable educational tool and may be even a rewarding hobby; but, like other things, it should not be made an obsession or a fad.

It used to be argued that the value of studying certain formal subjects like Latin and mathematics could be transferred to other quite different subjects and situations in life. Today it is known that, except under special conditions, very little of such transfer takes place. Mere utility has often been a cause for the condemnation of subjects of study. Shorthand has not escaped this criticism, partly because faddists have claimed too much for it, and partly because it has been looked upon as strictly vocational and of no educational value. What has not been realized is that shorthand works through the medium of language and for many students is often a key to its understanding. Moreover, shorthand, like many other vocational subjects, has other educative values in its effect on temperament, standards of work, and attitude of mind.

Just as reading and writing and a knowledge of numbers are necessary for the child to pass from the primary stage to the stage of self-help in education, so is the knowledge and practice of shorthand a key to progress in office work besides being useful as a personal asset. It is a part of office work which, unlike the routine of the accounts department and the everyday office practice, cannot be acquired through the normal routine of the office worker. It must be acquired before entry is made into practical affairs, or, if simultaneously with office work, then in evening or part-time schools, and, in consequence, it rightly forms an important part in the commercial curriculum.

Matter and Method

Again, it is not so much the matter as the method that counts in education; but, in general, matter and method cannot be divorced. Broad principles and theories of education can be laid down; but the teacher is called upon to select his method to suit his matter. The teacher of history follows lines different from those used by the teacher of mathematics; yet the fundamental theory is the same.

Do not let the young teacher, or the old one for that matter, hesitate at the idea of *theory* in education. Those without training in teaching are apt to consider theory as ideal and visionary or, at any rate, nebulous. Ideal it certainly is, but it is scientific and based on principles which, as knowledge increases, are constantly shifting and becoming more defined. The methods of today are not those of yesterday and our theory must always be in advance of practice. The decision of today may contradict that of yesterday if superior knowledge and research demands, as, for instance, the modern idea of *writing* shorthand characters as compared with the idea of laboriously drawing them, and the idea of aiming at speed from the beginning (with necessary safeguards) as opposed to theory first and speed only when the whole theory is mastered.

Educational Theory

Educational theory is not something to be read and forgotten, but is something to be assimilated and something upon which practice must be founded. It is impossible for one not trained in the principles of education to examine a method of teaching critically, and so it is not right for such a practitioner to reject a new method because he acquired the knowledge of his subject in some other way. He must make himself familiar with the principles underlying educational theory before rejecting progressive ideas, and, in the meantime, let him test the methods that have been used successfully by others.

Unfortunately, until quite recently, the business of training teachers of commercial subjects has been neglected, except in isolated cases, and methods of teaching have not been progressive. The student has become a teacher, and, in his turn, has adopted the only method that he knows, that of his own teacher. This is handed down through decades, and what was up to date forty years ago is in some places in vogue today. We have seen that theory is progressive, and practice must follow if the best results are to be obtained. The provision for the proper training of teachers of commercial subjects is beginning to receive more attention but is still very inadequate.

Psychology and the Teacher

An elementary knowledge of psychology is useful to the teacher, but it is not educational theory. The young teacher need have no fear either of the word or what it stands for. It is only a small part of the science that is of practical use to teachers, but that which is useful is of great value. If we are to teach John, then we should "know John." Knowing John means knowing something of John's mind or mental make-up. As we proceed, a slight sketch of the manner in which psychology assists pedagogy will be indicated. Just such a knowledge of psychology is needed as will help the teacher to see when a method is fundamentally wrong. Psychology simply lays down fundamental rules on the action of the mind in varying circumstances. Using these rules educationists postulate what should be done, how it should be done, and the reasons for doing it. These are arrived at, sometimes empirically by "trial and error" or "trial and success," but more often by the careful scientific inquiry and experiment of Institutes of Education. Educational theory is related to psychology in much the same way as hygiene and cookery are related to physiology. One can be a good cook without being a student of physiology; but it is well to understand something of the digestive organs.

CHAPTER II

LEARNING APPLIED TO SKILLS

THIS chapter deals with the processes of learning as they operate in acquiring skills. It is not so long ago that only academic learning was accounted worth serious study, but this attitude has largely disappeared. Today skills are respectable. As technological advance proceeds, the need for first-class skill training in ever-wider fields of activity becomes more urgent.

We learn for a variety of reasons, but one valid and necessary reason is that we must learn in order to equip ourselves to work for a living.

Levels of Mental Activity

In office work there are two kinds of mental activity demanded, namely, the activities of routine duties and those that need reasoning and judgment. It is the duty of the teacher of commercial subjects to train his students so that both these activities are developed on right lines. Routine activities must be so trained that they become very largely automatic, requiring little or no conscious thought. The highly trained secretary, who can copy-type speedily while she is talking to you about last night's play, is, in fact, performing the typing automatically, and leaving her higher mental activity free for the discussion of the play. Nobody can really "do two things at once" in the sense of exercising conscious thought and judgment on two things. The automatic activities in life, such as dressing, walking, washing, and, later, typing, shorthand writing, writing, spelling, adding, filing, and a hundred other items in the day's routine, are the concern, shall we say, roughly of the lower brain and upper spinal cord. It is our business as teachers to see that the upper brain or thinking part of the mental outfit is not too much concerned with these things, but is free for solving unusual problems, and giving consideration to those aspects of the subject matter of the skills that require intelligence, thought and mental application. The function of the teacher of shorthand is, therefore, an important one.

Flow of Nervous Energy

For the sake of simplifying matters, we may illustrate roughly what takes place in the nervous system when something external produces action in the pupil. It must be remembered that space does not permit of any long scientific analysis, nor can the accompanying diagram be said to be anything in the nature of a scientific chart.

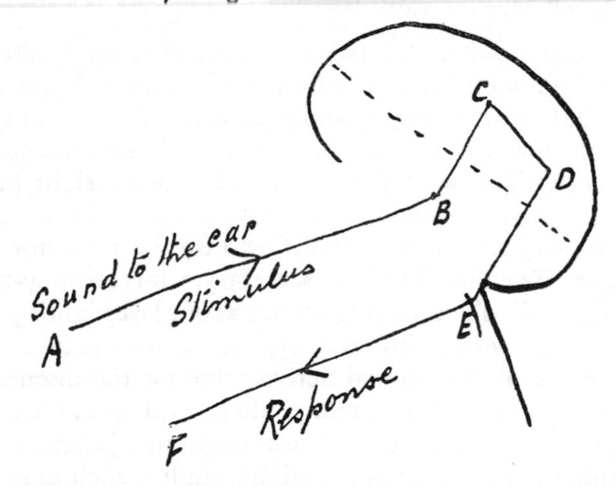

It is merely a simple sketch intended to convey some idea of the process of nervous activity.

The pupil has a stimulus *A* from without when the

teacher dictates a word. The stimulus through the ear is recorded at a nerve centre *B* situated in the lower brain. This communicates with another nerve centre *C* in the upper brain, where it is sorted, labelled and passed on to a further centre *D*, which commands the response. Finally, the response is made through the centre *E*, which controls the muscles of the hand, and the result is that the outline representing the word is written.

Now it may be seen that both parts of the brain are used on this occasion. Something happens along the path taken, and we know from experience that the more often the process is repeated, using the same stimulus, the quicker is the response, and we may assume that this quickness is due to the fact that some kind of a track is made until the response comes more readily, and requires less and less work from the higher centres of mental activity. That is, conscious thinking is not required. It is the job of the teacher of all formal subjects to short-circuit the track, so that stimulus and response come along from *A* to *B*, *B* to *E*, *E* to *F*, leaving the upper brain to be called upon only for new emergencies. This may be an unscientific way of putting the matter, but it will help to make the teaching situation clearer.

Stimulus-response Bonds

The brain and spinal cord contain numerous nerve centres, and if the stimulus connects with the wrong centre the response will be wrong. It is the teacher's business to see that the *original* response is right; hence the importance of securing *correct theoretical outlines* carefully written from the start. It is a good device for the teacher to adopt the method of familiarizing his students with new outlines and difficult outlines likely to give trouble *before* dictating a new piece to beginners in the speed room (see page 119). Indeed, there is much to commend the practice of restricting "free" dictating, at any rate in the early stages of speed development, very largely to passages that have already been read, re-read, copied, and read from the shorthand note. Another plan is to dictate a piece at a speed well within the power of the pupil, and then during the following lesson to dictate the same piece at the maximum speed of the class. In a further lesson the rate of reading *of the same piece* may again be raised (see page 118). Short forms may be taught in the same way on a sound psychological basis of forming a pathway for the stimulus of sound through the appropriate nerve centres to the muscles of the hand. In the teaching of Pitman's shorthand, thousands of these pathways are to be made. We can look upon the writing of an outline or a shorthand symbol as the result of a bond between the stimulus and the response, that is, between the spoken word and the act of recording it. Indeed the modern psychologist speaks of the connexion, mentally made, as a *stimulus-response bond*. Each new word or sequence of words that we record has its own new bond, and that is why a certain mental hesitancy is observed due to the groping for the rule and the working of the higher mental equipment. It is the teacher's sphere to employ those methods most likely to eliminate this unnecessary stage.

If the theory expounded on pages 11 to 14 is accepted, then we can safely say that "practice makes perfect" (page 40); and if we can obtain such perfection in the writing of the common words of the language we are making progress towards shorthand perfection. In the textbook of Pitman's shorthand called *A Modern Course in Pitman's Shorthand* this principle is applied to the method of presentation. The examples given and the exercises to be worked are selected on a common-word basis, and as the work proceeds common phrases and words are met with over and over again until the student has written them so often in context that they are at his pen point immediately they are spoken. These 700 words with their derivatives supply some 80 per cent of normal English (pages 76–82). A similar principle with some extension of vocabulary up to about 1,200 words is to be found in the *New Course*.

Combining modern views with earlier ideas, we can say that the principles of teaching are based on simple laws which must be clearly understood and applied by every teacher. The ancient told us to relate the new to the old, the modern speaks of "the law of interest"; "practice makes perfect" was the old precept, but we now speak more commonly of the "law of use." Without using any but simple technical terms already explained, we may say that the three most important essentials to learning are—

1. A mind properly prepared and continuously applied (the law of readiness).
2. The making and remaking of stimulus-response bonds (the law of use).
3. A continuing feeling of satisfaction as a result of 1 and 2 (the law of effect).

We now pass to a consideration of these essentials.

Consciousness

There is no such thing as a mind wholly blank, but it may be that in a state of relaxation there is no one particular thing on which the thoughts are dwelling; nevertheless, there is always, during waking hours and in dreams, and, maybe, at other times, a state of consciousness. Consciousness is the knowledge of the existence of a mental state indicated by our feelings, desires, hopes, deliberations. It is unstable, showing a background of generalities and maybe some particularity in the foreground which is constantly changing. It may be likened to the view seen from a rapidly moving train; near objects pass and are replaced by others, whilst the distance changes only gradually until we rush into a tunnel and out again into a new vista.

Consciousness comes in pulses, and how it comes about is not the subject of the teacher's inquiry. It is due to a combination drawn from out of the experiences that have been our lot in life, and no two persons have exactly the same wave operating at the same moment. Even difference in clothes, health, age, religious feeling and everything that differentiates one human being from another affects the pulses of consciousness that constantly flow through us. They consist of memories of past experience, present happenings, feelings of comfort or discomfort, desires and fears, and, in fact, all the emotions. If a distracting noise prevents our reading in comfort, the strength of the pulse of consciousness or the centre of the field at the moment is the distraction or its cause, whilst all other matters are a kind of margin or dimly-conceived background. The noise passes, and the story we are reading becomes the centre of our field of consciousness, having in its background or on its margin or fringe the matters which are raised by the story itself, the past happenings that are recalled, and the like. There is a constant change taking place in both the focus and in the margin of consciousness. Sometimes the focus remains somewhat constant, and this is due to interest and attention. Sometimes the focus changes and marginal consciousness comes into focus. In the middle of a shorthand lesson, when the subject-matter has been in focus and the outside distractions, such as street noises, movements of restless students, the rustling of books, spasmodic coughing, have been on the margin, there may be sudden changes of focus because a radio has been switched on, or a pile of books has fallen to the floor. Then the margin comes into focus and the subject-matter of the lesson becomes marginal.

It is the teacher's aim to secure attention, to bring the lesson into clear-cut focus, and to keep it there. This is his greatest task. Without success in this aim his efforts have been in vain, and unless he can secure this attention his teaching will fail. The teacher is teaching only when the students are learning, and the students can learn only when attention is focused and interest is present.

All this may seem extremely nebulous; indeed it is, and the psychologist does not help us very much. The enthusiasm, energy and personal qualities of the teacher are most important.

Stimulus and Reaction

Every stimulus from without so affects the person stimulated that there is a natural response. Just as in the physical sciences it is claimed that every action has its reaction, so in a consideration of the mental effect of a stimulus we claim a corresponding reaction. The prick of a pin produces muscular movement and possibly articulation. The sight of misery may produce tears; an accident may cause sickness in the observer; a rebuke administered to a pupil, as a stimulus coming to the nerve centre through the ear, may cause shame and the reaction may be seen in a blush; or the effect may be to cause the pupil to put restraint on the tongue—a form of negative reaction; but no impression is received into the mental outfit without corresponding expression which is not, however, necessarily overt. This is simply illustrated in the diagram on page 12, where the psychological principle is followed to its pedagogical conclusion. Unless the expression follows, there is no effect on memory and the experience is not woven into the mental make-up. It is the *doing* of something, the sensation of acting, either positively or negatively, that fixes the impression.

In teaching shorthand, when an example is given, let it be written by the students—a good blackboard during a lesson means nothing unless the student has also a good notebook. The writing is the expression of the impression received by the eye or the ear. A description of an outline produces vagueness; the writing of it produces exactness.

Law of Effect

Remember that the cycle of activity is not complete when the student has made his outline. He has the knowledge of having acted, and this produces a sensation of satisfaction or dissatisfaction. The result of his action affects other people, and it is a human trait to care what the observer thinks of our acts. The student needs encouragement and friendly admonition, guidance and intelligent correction. He needs to be continuously aware of progress and of the particular targets he is aiming at, at any stage during his instruction. From all this he will derive a continuing satisfaction and sustained interest. The notebooks should be seen by the teacher, otherwise the student has a sense of incompleteness and his work deteriorates. Many teachers fail to recognize that *notes or outlines taken by way of example* and explanation of a rule *are as important as the exercise* that is dictated, and if neglected a wholly inadequate style of writing may be the result.

CHAPTER III

ATTENTION AND INTEREST

THE acceptance of the truth that consciousness comes to us in a succession of waves, or in complete fields, which are undergoing constant change warns us that our task is to secure for the whole lesson something approaching fixity in a particular wave or field. We have seen that the process of change is rapid when interests are rapidly aroused, and that attention to a given matter depends on interest. The motive underlying all our conduct is interest in its widest sense, and the thing most interesting to us is most likely to claim our attention. The function of the teacher is to arouse interest and so secure attention to the problem under consideration.

Interest

The term *interest* is in reality a technical one, for, as used here, it has a wider meaning than is popularly understood. If a man particularly wants to catch a certain train in order that he may keep an important business appointment, and his time is short, his whole interest is centred on the train and the time. The opening buds in his well-loved garden have no attraction; the headline posters of the morning paper are passed unheeded; and he may miss the cheery "Good Morning" of those whom he is accustomed to greet, or, at any rate, his greeting may be so automatic that he may, at a later time, be unable to recollect what persons he met on his journey to the station. The whole of his mental energy is focused on the one interesting thing, the 8.30 train.

The boy who falls whilst carrying a bottle of milk is

interested only in the accident and its consequences. The game which was instrumental in causing the catastrophe has lost interest; no doubt the object of real interest is the excuse which must necessarily be made. Interest, for our purpose, is defined by Dr. Franklin Jones as "a feeling of usefulness of objects as a means of realizing a present purpose." Thus the umbrella left behind becomes interesting at the first spot of rain; the bus is interesting when its arrival brings us nearer to the evening meal; the newspaper that gives the result of the cup tie is interesting; and so on through an unending list. It might be objected that some of these things are doubtful as *useful* objects; but again we must widen our view of usefulness and accept the idea that a thing is *useful to us* if it is a means to achieve *our ends*, irrespective of the value of the ends in the opinion of others.

Our end is to teach our students to record the speech of other persons rapidly and accurately, and Pitman's shorthand is the *useful object* which is a means of realizing that purpose. Immediately this is conceded, interest is aroused in the subject, and what American writers call the *law of readiness* comes into play.

Instinct

Where does interest come from? If we examine the cases mentioned, the traveller and the train, the boy and the broken milk bottle, or if we think of the interest of a hungry man, namely, food, or of the interest of the mother of a sick child, we see that interest is founded or based on instinct. It is, therefore, to instinct that we appeal if we wish to arouse interest.

The most predominant of human instincts is that of self-preservation. Food, warmth, comfort, shelter are all dear to the human species, and the teacher of vocational subjects has at hand the means of arousing interest in his subjects. Do not be afraid of using the motive at hand as a means of preparing your pupils for their course of lessons. The interest once aroused, the law of readiness comes into play. Keep it in play by making your exercises practical. Get to work on real words and real conversation as quickly as possible. Get your words into reasonable sentences as soon as may be, and dictate sound, sensible letters, so that the practical value of your subject may always remain before your class. Rouse them by insisting on the *reality* of what you are teaching, not by talking but by doing.

In considering the question of interest in general, it must be remembered that the teacher has many enemies in and out of the classroom. The native instincts of the students, though not so strongly marked in older pupils as in younger ones, have to be reckoned with and utilized by the teacher. It is not possible, in this slight sketch of the psychological view of interest, to show how native instincts are utilized in primary teaching. It is sufficient to note that even older pupils find distraction in living things, in realities and in the drama. These are *real* interests; but we are at a stage in teaching when *artificial* interests are to be cultivated. The connexion can be made by good use of the blackboard or by the telling of an appropriate story. The writer has been impressed by the success of the teacher who was naturally humorous in his selection of examples and in their use; but this is a personal matter capable of adoption only by those whose gifts lie in that direction.

Association

From what has been discussed already of the way in which nervous energy flows, we can conclude that the total effect is from impression to reaction and from reaction to result, which in itself is a stimulus producing further reaction. Without thinking in technical terms, each one of us comes to associate the various elements one with another, and we come to expect certain results from certain impressions. This association is the mainspring of teaching.

Laws of Association

Psychologists are not in agreement as to the true inwardness of association, so that we as teachers must accept it without using up our time in endeavouring to discover its causes. That it follows certain laws is admitted, and it is on the basis of these laws that the teacher must work. Successive fields of consciousness are in some way related to each other. The rattle of cups on a bright sunny day may recall to mind a pleasant picnic of years ago, and the fruit and cream that appealed to us on that occasion; and this may remind us of the larder and of the cream that must be eaten before it becomes uneatable. The laws of contiguity, similarity and contrast are the basic laws of associative sequence. One sees this clearly in the integral part played in language by such figurative elements as personification, metaphor, simile, and metonymy. But we may avoid technical terms and accept the conclusion that our pupils are fitted with a mental make-up which works naturally when it is associating and relating one thing with another. It is natural for us to see faces in the fire and to have day dreams in times of relaxation. Indeed the dreamy pupil who indulges in flights of fancy may well, with proper guidance, be one who is easily taught through association.

The teacher's problem is to adjust himself to three important truths, namely—

1. Association is the main cause of the mind's functioning.
2. Interest decides the course of the mind's functioning.
3. Attention prevents the mind from useless straying.

Metaphorically, association is the motive power, interest is the veering wind, whilst attention is the firm hand at the helm.

Variety of Associations

The mind is so constituted that the sight of a given object or the sound of a word will commence a train of thought which will end none knows where. The endings will not bear any semblance in the case of any two in a group of persons, unless they have been together under similar circumstances or under circumstances which cause the same associative train. Thus a rose to one may bring up a garden seen on a June holiday with all its related experience; to another it may recall a dress worn by an almost forgotten friend; to another the scent may bring the memory of a room where some well-remembered scene was enacted; and then quickly follows the recollection of the results of an interview, or the like. In each case, the rose, the cause of these quickly changing fields of consciousness, may be forgotten. Of what value is this to the teacher of shorthand? Firstly, it is his aim to see that the associated ideas of each person in the class before him are as far as possible the same. He must be ready to steer the mind in the direction along which it is desirable for the thought of his pupils to travel. He must arouse interest in the subject and claim his pupils' attention, as we have already indicated.

Ideas cannot exist in the mind as single units, but only in associated groups; and the more links that a given idea makes, the better is it retained and the more easily is it recalled.

Grouping of Ideas

Throughout conscious life we go on receiving impressions. The teacher would do well to remember that all experience comes to us primarily through the senses, and especially through sight and hearing. Previous impressions determine the present mental attitude of our students. These previous impressions, which are the sum total of life's experience, do not exist in the mind in an incoherent fashion, but they have mutual relationship. One impression entering the mind links up with another. The teacher who can facilitate this linking helps the new ideas to find a permanent resting-place in the mind.

Opportunities for the grouping of ideas are numerous, and several apparently unrelated groups may be very firmly connected. If a thought cannot be called up in one way, try another. The cue you first use may fail, but another may obtain the desired result. Vary the wording of your questions and your illustrations. In recapitulation and your revision lessons avoid the examples given in your introductory lessons. It is on this principle that the complete revision of theoretical knowledge given in *The Student's Review* is based. It offers new dictation exercises and a new view of the rules. The writer remembers an occasion upon which, after a lesson on the hooks included in the circles, the question was put "Under what circumstances can the sound of *n* be represented by a large hook?" As theory it was immaterial, but as an associative device it was useful to remind the students that the large circle in words like *tenses*, *dances*, *chances* included the *n* hook, which, in such words, is naturally larger than when it is included in the small circle in tense, dance, chance, and similar words. It is merely a new point of view in association with older ideas.

If the foregoing is kept in mind, the teacher will have a more open mind in regard to what sometimes seems the stupidity of the student. He will realize that the answer he associates with his questions may not be anything like that which the student returns and that if this is so, wrong association of ideas has developed. At a later stage something will be said on the art of questioning.

Law of Preparation

The Herbartian principle of "preparation for the new lesson" is based upon the laws of association. It is not sufficient to tell the class the nature of the problem before it; we must relate the problem to what is already known. Thus in a first lesson on the *shun* hook—

1. Refer to alternative forms for *s*, *st*, the hooks and strokes for *n*, *f*, *v*, *r* and *l* when these are in appropriate conjunction. Speedily revise the final hooks.

2. Obtain from the students a list of words ending in *-sion*, *-tion*, *-cian*, etc.

3. Now introduce the alternative form for the combination *sh-n*, i.e. the *shun* hook.

4. Finally suggest that the problem is to apply the alternative in appropriate cases, showing how the device has the effect of abbreviating the outline and adding to facility.

The direction of the hook is found in its own name *shun*, meaning "to avoid or keep clear of." Thus we have a mnemonic (page 55) which helps us with three of the four rules relating to the direction of the hook. The hook *shuns* the side of the initial attachment to a straight stroke; it *shuns* the side of the curves *f* and *v* followed by a straight stroke; and finally it *shuns* the side of the simple straight stroke where the last sounded vowel is found.

There is only one other rule dealing with the direction of the hook, namely, that the hook is on the right of the perpendicular strokes *t* and *d*, the opposite side to the one taken by the hook *n*.

Danger in Memory Devices

Do not forget that there may be danger in these devices. Slow-witted people have been known to represent that something which is an accident, and which serves merely as a memory aid has been deliberately planned. The *shun* hook, of course, has no real relationship to the English verb "to shun"; but the accidental relationship is a useful example of methods of utilizing association, the grafting of the new upon the old.

To sum up the present chapter, interest is essential to promote learning, and, properly handled, uninteresting things may acquire an interest. Interest is in action rather than in words, and it may be aroused by *doing* and by associating new things with old ones in a meaningful way. Remember that voluntary attention is transient and not sustained, and that constant stimulation is necessary to keep attention from wandering. The noisy teacher cannot keep attention. It may be necessary on occasion to raise the voice; but this should not become habitual, or it loses any value that it might once have had.

Interest wanes if methods are stereotyped and, consequently, attention wanders. Study the various methods of teaching and use them all, as appropriate. Variety in attack keeps the allies, *attention* and *interest*, alive; and, finally, remember that new things are difficult to learn unless they are connected with those things that are already in mind. What is understood only dimly at first, must be made clearer and more precise by recapitulation during the lesson, and revision afterwards. Otherwise interest will wane through frustration and lack of success. Knowledge of progress and the realization of success are powerful agents in sustaining interest at a high level.

CHAPTER IV

MAKING USE OF INSTINCTIVE BEHAVIOUR

In the previous chapter we accepted the psychological view that interest was founded on instinct. Whilst it is not necessary to enter fully into the question of instinct, it is well to observe that certain native instincts are present in all human creatures, and many of these may be utilized as a means of holding attention and securing the will to learn, which is discipline. For the teacher of adolescents the most important is the group of instincts which William James has called the *ambition impulses*. They are five in number and are closely related. Starting with *imitation*, they pass through *emulation* to *ambition*, and are connected with *pride* and *pugnacity*. To these add the instincts of *curiosity* and of *the desire to please* those whom we respect, and we have a starting-point from which the teacher can do much. Fear is an instinct which ought never, or very rarely, to be used by the teacher as an instrument.

Imitation

Imitation has always been recognized as one of the primary instincts of man, and modern psychologists recognize its importance to the extent of whole chapters and works on the subject. Success in teaching any subject in which muscular activity is needed is dependent on the imitative faculty. We illustrate our lesson by examples, and we call upon our students to "do that." Having shown them "how," we expect them to imitate us. If their interest is fully secured, we shall find them doing it as we did it, even to the incorporation of our own peculiarities. It is well, therefore, before we stand before the blackboard, that we should make ourselves familiar with blackboard technique. We should be careful about our outlines and endeavour to secure that they are in proportion to the surface at our disposal. If, for purposes of illustration, we adopt the useful but not unusual plan of making large and bold symbols, let us make it clear that these are for one purpose only. "Let me make that large enough for everyone to see it" should be our introduction to such an illustration, and then, for purposes of imitation, we can write it of normal size.

When making use of the imitative instinct in skill teaching, we should be careful not only that what is seen is imitated but also that the correct movements in space and time are imitated. Developing the awareness of the kinaesthetic sense is important in teaching shorthand and typewriting.

Emulation

The point where emulation begins and imitation ceases is not easy to ascertain, for, with the adolescent, the teacher who is loved is emulated, and the student whose personality makes for leadership is copied by his admirers. This fact should be of value in class tuition. Even older students are pleased to have their shorthand penmanship or fair copy displayed as something achieved and to be emulated. The display board should find a prominent place in the shorthand classroom, but it should be used judiciously and generally only for the best examples of a student's work. Again, your own shorthand outlines by way of correction in the students' notebooks should be carefully executed, as they are intended as a pattern to be followed. No correction should be made and left there;

but the student should be called upon to rewrite and drill on the corrected outline. It is a wise plan in the theory stage to use alternate lines of the notebook when taking down exercises in shorthand—

1st line. Student's shorthand in ink (black) and teacher's corrections in ink (red).

2nd line. Blank for rewriting the whole exercise as fair copy.

3rd line. Shorthand as dictated, and so on.

The *Combined Notebook and Exercises* for use with the *Shorthand Commercial Course* is compiled on this plan. The longhand exercise for writing in shorthand is printed in this book, and longhand writing is thus reduced to a minimum. Two blank lines are left after the printed copy; the first line is for the student's exercise in shorthand, the second being used after the first is corrected for a correct fair copy.

The teacher who writes well and with facility on the blackboard is a great assistance to a class. Even more important is his ability to write a light, small, quick, controlled style in ink when demonstrating in a shorthand notebook to a small group of students. What he does with ease is admired and students emulate it. It is a concrete case of example being better than precept.

Exceeding Oneself

Whilst we moderns cannot accept Rousseau's dictum that Emile should not compare himself with his fellows, we can go part of the way with him and call upon our pupils to exceed themselves. Progress recorded and compared, with a cheery word and a helping hand to the weaklings, is well worth while. "Your exercises this week are much better than last week's" will probably produce its results in further striving. On the other hand, public reprobation of adolescent and senior students cannot do any good, as it generally damps enthusiasm, which is fatal to interest. There is no rule of educational theory that applies to the utilization of the native instinctive trait of emulation. Sympathy and tact will work upon the pupils' feelings and rouse the instinct that is akin to love. It is then a case for the teacher of clinching matters. If the student can be brought to see that he is capable of doing at least some work as well as the best student in the class, he is on the way to emulating the best in other respects also.

Encouragement the Key-note of Teaching

Freedom from worry and a mind at peace is essential to good shorthand work. The nagging teacher is his own and his pupils' worst enemy. He should remember that irony and sarcasm are injurious. Of the three laws that have been mentioned, namely, preparation, use and effect, the law of effect plays an important part in the fixing of shorthand outlines. The student who has a feeling of well-being and pleasure as a result of a thing well done is likely to repeat that thing; and, on the other hand, a feeling of dissatisfaction caused by the pupil's own indifferent work or by his failure to please his teacher, is likely to prove an impediment in the way of the free flow of nervous energy in the future. Our impulses usually culminate in action; but, if two impressions are present, namely, the impression which produces an impulse to act in a certain way, and a further impression whose corresponding expression is a restraining action, then inhibition may be stronger than the impulse, or it may weaken the impulse so that the expression (in our case the written shorthand outline) is imperfect and uncertain. Encouragement is the key-note to all teaching, but the reader must not think that this means a belief in a gentle, leisurely, sentimentally false kind of a classroom technique.

Ambition Impulses

Ambition, pride and pugnacity, together with envy and jealousy, are the selfish instincts, and, whilst they can be morally dangerous, they are natural instincts on which a teacher can make a start. As teaching appeals they must be refined. Ambition may be used to encourage in achievement; the girl who starts life as a shorthand writer may become the secretary of her company, a star verbatim reporter. Pugnacity and pride again are egoistic impulses, very properly appealed to in the classroom. The spirit of unwillingness to be defeated is worthy of being fostered, and this is really what pugnacity is. Often the best that is in a pupil can be roused by the appeal that what others have done under difficult circumstances should not be a stumbling-block to one of his calibre. Pugnacity and pride are the instincts that ensure the healthy rivalry which is an asset in class teaching. It is good that the best student shall be the pacemaker for the rest of the class, but never to the detriment of the naturally slow mover, who requires our help and encouragement at every step. The teacher has a difficult and important task, for the 100 per cent are his care; and, though his name may be made by the phenomenal results obtained by the few, he himself is satisfied, and he is the bigger man, if the many owe to him their progress and success. Classes can never be entirely homogeneous and teachers will often find that they must strike a balance between two essentials—the need to draw the best out of the quick, clever students, and the need to guide, help and foster the pride and will to learn of the least gifted in the class.

Curiosity as an Aid

Curiosity, like other human instincts, is in its narrow sense bad, but in the wider sense, as the impulse directing towards a better knowledge of life's experiences, it is by far the most educative of all the instincts. Every new impression excites the curiosity. At first this is so in material things, in action, in living things; but later in abstract things. By the time our pupils come to us in the commercial schools, curiosity in the abstract is possible, and curiosity alone is sufficient to arouse interest in the new form of writing that is placed before them. The instinct of curiosity can be used by the teacher in that very important training in shorthand reading—a task often neglected, but as important to success as shorthand writing. Let the reading be interesting; recommend your students to make use of the many interesting stories now produced in printed shorthand for their use.

Curiosity is the seeking after reasons and causes, and it is aroused more by a new aspect of a known thing or fact than by something to which we are accustomed. This is the main reason for the reminder that *interest may be challenged by new methods and new approach.* The boy or girl who passes a window daily without more than an interested glance is one day attracted by something that was not there before—a cat amongst the coats, an overturned flower vase, a brightly coloured and attractive poster or a mechanical advertising device. It is the teacher's business in his shorthand lesson to manufacture devices and to arouse curiosity anew. Take particular pains to arouse curiosity at the beginning of a lesson, and keep the students alert and curious by introducing variety of approach and avoiding a stereotyped lesson pattern.

Motive the Root of Interest

The teacher of commercial subjects, if a practical man of affairs, engaged in the realities of business life, may well ask to what end this theorizing; but he will gradually come to see its value if he pursues the theory to the end, and try to know his students just as he knows the subject which he wishes them to make their own. Let him realize that *interest is founded on instinct, attention on interest, and that instinct is not called into play without motive*; he will then begin to see his own connexion with all that has been said.

The native instincts are called into play only when need arises, and, as the native instincts are the foundation upon which the teacher builds, it is necessary for him to show to his students the use of his subject before he can secure their interest. Let them see the end, and the beginning is made more easy, for, to sum up this part of our subject, in non-technical language, we may say that, given the need, instinct is aroused, interest, as defined in the previous chapter, follows, attention is secured, and *the law of preparedness comes into action.* Motivation may properly begin at the humble level of the incentive to acquire a skill of direct £ s. d. value in everyday life. It may move to higher levels in which there are the additional motives of giving service to the best of one's ability, of the desire to excel as an end in itself—to climb Everest because it is there to climb.

Apperception

Before considering *the law of use*, or, as our less technical forebears had it, "practice makes perfect," we will consider the manner in which new ideas are assimilated by the learner; and here we are confronted by a technical word.

Apperception is really a very simple thing, a name given

to a state of things well known to teachers long before the word was coined. William James tells us that it means nothing more than "the act of taking a thing into the mind." An idea is apperceived when it links itself with other ideas already a part of the mental make-up, and, naturally, the significance of the new things will depend entirely on the old things already known.

A child who has seen birds but never an aeroplane will, from his limited ideas, take in the new phenomenon and link it with the flying creatures that he already knows. The older person sees in it an aeroplane; another apperceives it as a jet-liner; another delta wing pressurised World Airways aircraft; and so on. Thus we *perceive* a thing as outside ourselves by sight, touch, etc., that is, through sensation, and next we relate it to things within our mental make-up, that is, we *apperceive* it, and finally, coming to know the general class to which the thing apperceived belongs, we form a *concept* or, less technically, a complete idea. We shall see the value of this when we come to the subject of the method of reasoning.

We have already learned that ideas do not exist separately in the mind, but are linked in groups. Each group may be considered as an apperceiving mass into which new ideas are constantly being received. It is the business of the teacher to see that these apperceiving masses are properly constituted. In the teaching of abstract things, clearness of description and definition is essential, or the new idea to be taught may become linked in the wrong group. Remember that all knowledge is arrived at by building up concepts out of percepts—in plain English, by arriving at general conclusions through the examination of individual cases. If the percepts are wrongly apperceived, the conclusions will be wrong. Thus a child sees and knows a ball. Suppose it sees an orange for the first time. This is outside its experience, and it apperceives it as a ball. Now if the orange be cut and the child, not having reached the investigation stage, has never cut a ball or seen a ball cut, it may reasonably conclude that the inside of a ball bears a resemblance to that of an orange. The danger of arriving at a general notion derived from wrong apperception or from an inadequate number of instances is great. In your teaching, therefore, *let your examples be copious before asking your class to frame a general rule.*

Fear

Fear, too, is an immensely powerful instinct which has been called into use in the past as a factor in teaching. Today, there is some plain advice that emerges from all educational psychology—never resort to fear as an agent in teaching. Fear is one of the ugliest and most damaging of all instincts in an educational context, and can never, under any circumstances, produce any desired result of education.

CHAPTER V

LAW OF USE

We now come to consider more fully the second law of learning, namely, the law of use. This is of vital importance in our subject, but it is very dependent on preparedness. We have already seen that every external stimulus creating a mental impression, whether through the eye, the ear, the nose or the skin, is followed by its corresponding expression. "There can be no reception without reaction; there can be no impression without expression." We have further seen how the circuit of nervous energy is set up in the creation of stimulus-response bonds, and it is now our business to examine the question of making these bonds automatically or without *conscious* thought. In other words, our next business is to consider the question of habit formation.

Are Habits Desirable?

It is first necessary to consider whether the formation of habit is, or is not, desirable. It has been pointed out by other writers that the word "habits" generally suggests bad habits; but we should remember that there are good as well as bad automatic actions. Habits are essential, although the man who becomes entirely a creature of habit becomes limited in his outlook, and depreciated in his value to himself and to his employers. It follows, therefore, that, in the formation of habits, precautions are necessary. In our ordinary lives there are numerous daily actions which should become more or less a matter of habit—dressing, shaving, walking, going up and down stairs—and such routine parts of our lives become possible because they are more or less automatic. The principle that should be adopted in matters which are really of small account, and which have often to be repeated is to let them become habitual, but to ensure that the habit developed is the most economical and efficient for its purpose. Where great importance might be attached to actions, they should not be too fully automatized. For instance, in these days of traffic difficulties, whilst walking is automatic, such walking as is used in crossing the road should receive thought and attention, not so much for the actual movements, but from the point of view of decision as to when the movements should be made. In teaching such subjects as writing, spelling, calculating, typewriting and shorthand, this is a problem of great importance.

Reflex Action

In the writing of shorthand the student performs a series of muscular reactions resultant upon an external stimulus. Gradually a trackway is formed in the manner suggested in a previous chapter. This way becomes so easily followed that, given the necessary external impulse, the succeeding conduct becomes practically reflex. Reflex actions are those which take place without conscious knowledge. Thus a child grips an object placed near the palm of its hand without giving conscious thought to the object itself. Certain other human traits are reflex in their character—sucking, crying, blushing, frowning, coughing, all of which are, to a certain extent, independent of volition or conscious effort.

Habit is said to be second nature, and this is, in a measure, true. If we consider that the native human instincts are "first nature," then the habits that have been superimposed may be looked upon as "second nature." It is not the moral aspect, important though this is, that must claim our attention at this point. It is rather the physical response that must be considered.

Thought and Habitual Actions

The formation of habits which are necessary in penmanship, whether longhand or shorthand, is a matter of the creation of stimulus-response bonds; and, as in all other forms of teaching, the teacher who is endeavouring to cultivate habits should make his methods of teaching conform to the three laws that have already been mentioned. The law of use, which means that once a stimulus-response bond is created it is easier to use the same path again than to form a new one, is the very essence of habit formation. The first rule, therefore, in forming a habit is to allow no exceptions. The well-known analogy of the ball of string is useful; remember that it takes a considerable time to wind a ball of string; but, let it slip through the fingers, it very rapidly unwinds, and, in order to re-wind it, more has to be undone to take in the slack. It is not a question of beginning winding where you left off, but of going back over old ground. This is sometimes put forward as a reason for teachers refraining from altering their methods; but there is a considerable difference between changing horses in the middle of the stream and changing horses when you come to a new stream. Having commenced to teach your students one way of doing a thing, do not then tell them that you have found a better way, without very carefully considering the effect. You can try the better way with your next group of students.

Having acquired a form of response that is habitual, the student does not keep the rule in mind. The first time an outline is written it is written according to rule or example. On a second occasion it is easier to write; but still the rule or the copy is referred to. The more often it is repeated, the easier it becomes and the less is the rule in evidence. Repetition produces ease, because there is the actual making of a pathway in the nervous organism which allows the reaction to occur more easily. The speed with which shorthand outlines can be written eventually prevents the writer from referring to the rule. Indeed, it is certain that reference to a rule at high speed would cause mental hesitancy which would be fatal to success. There comes a time in the practice of high speed shorthand writing when increase in rapidity is a matter of penmanship and of familiarity, and not of shorthand.

The famous legend of the centipede and the toad illustrates the effect of too much thought being given to automatic movements—

The centipede was happy quite, until the toad for fun,
Said, "Pray, which leg goes after which?"
This brought his mind to such a pitch,
He lay distracted in a ditch,
Considering how to run.

Meaningful Repetition

Habits such as are built up in most formal subjects of the school curriculum are said to be of the sensory-motor type. These are formed by repetition and drill; but, as in every other branch of learning, interest is essential. "Practice makes perfect" when the practice is good and when the interest in it is sustained. If the necessary repetition and drill is to bring its full value, the student must know precisely what he is doing and why he is doing it. He must know the goal he is aiming at, and the length of time he has to reach it. He must have defined standards of attainment in mind, be self-critical, and aware of his personal failings. He must be making a continuous conscious effort of improvement, always under some reasonable pressure of time. Only in this way, when all these conditions are satisfied, can the drill produce a desired result. Otherwise repetition will result only in monotony, boredom, loss of interest and stagnation in achievement.

Progress in shorthand and typewriting is generally rapid at first, particularly when the work is class work, but there is often a slowing-off, which in evening classes results in, first, casual absence, and then, finally, total abstention. This is almost entirely due to the waning of interest, and interest should be maintained throughout. If students begin to stay away and the class dwindles, it is often too late to save the situation. Something will be said, when dealing with methods of teaching, of the ways in which this period of slackening progress can be avoided. Change of method and variety of activity is the best plan to adopt, avoiding routine and drudgery as much as possible. The best way to maintain interest is to let the student feel the satisfaction (the law of effect) of constant progression. The feeling that he is doing real work and that he is "getting somewhere" is one of the surest ways of maintaining the attention of a class. Hard work only becomes drudgery when motive and interest are absent.

With regard to habitual responses, the teacher should be aware of the fact that, because a student knows an outline, it does not necessarily follow that he will write it correctly. Writing shorthand is a matter of motor co-ordinations, and we must remember that the writing muscles are different from the group of muscles which control speech and the group which control sight. In either longhand or shorthand, the writing of familiar words is a matter of habit, and this accounts for the greatest percentage of errors in speed work. The mere fact that a pupil has written a certain small and apparently unimportant word many times causes him to write this word when he hears another of roughly similar sound, and writing may become so automatic that the wrong word may be written in a purely reflex way. These errors will not be seen at the lower speeds so much as at the higher. At 30, 40, and even 50 words per minute, a certain amount of what may be called conscious thinking is necessary, and writing is not yet automatic. At higher speeds it becomes more automatized, and more than 50 per cent of the errors made by shorthand speed writers are due to motor inco-ordinations, that is, the failure of the hearing group of nerves to co-ordinate with the writing group sufficiently quickly for the correct response to appear in writing. The only way to eliminate this type of error is self-correction. The student must be made aware of his fault and must correct his errors for himself, afterwards drilling on the outlines.

Two other teaching points concerned with habit need constant watchfulness. Establishing a good habit is as easy as establishing a bad one. Eradicating a bad habit is many times more difficult. It follows that it is vitally important to establish the right habits at the start. This is why all or almost all the shorthand material used during the learning period should be read and re-read, copied and re-copied before ever the student is called upon to write "free" dictation. What is known can be dictated. What is not known is unsuitable for dictation.

The second point is that habit formation applies just as much to the style as to the content of shorthand writing. Such concentration will be needed to establish the habits of writing shorthand very lightly and quickly, of writing small controlled strokes and outlines, uniform in size, of writing in the correct, fluent and cursive fashion.

CHAPTER VI

FUNDAMENTALS OF THE SKILL

THE great majority of the important points in the more efficient teaching of shorthand arise from a proper appreciation of the fundamental problem—that the teaching of shorthand is the problem of training a skill connected with the ear to co-ordinate itself with a second skill, also to be trained, which is connected with the muscles of the fingers; and then, as a separate function, to train a third skill, connected with the eye, to read back the results of the other two skills. Finally, these three skills are to be developed in the medium of the English language, a fact which in itself has important bearings on the methods of development of all of them.

Consider these three skills in turn, and the impact of all of them on the ascertainable peculiarities of the English language.

Training the Ear

The problem of getting the ear to develop the skill of associating an air-borne sound with a particular shorthand outline comes first. How is this skill to be developed? It is unnecessary to emphasize that this can be done only by giving the student a conception of the correct outline which is appropriate to a particular air-borne sound (which we call a spoken word) and keeping it constantly associated by repetition. First we must admit that dictation is the essential basis of this part of our function. Clearly, dictation must begin at the very beginning, and the words dictated must be those which the student has been taught, and therefore the teaching of outlines must immediately precede dictation. This is the justification of "preparation before dictation." Clearly, also, the writing of shorthand from the *written* word rather than from the spoken word does not at all—or at very best only indifferently—develop the skill of the ear. The longhand exercises in a textbook should be worked by the student not from the exercise book, but from the spoken word of the teacher, and it must be borne in mind that, if you allow your students to work from the printed word, you are developing a skill of the eye in associating the particular ether-borne image of a black mark on paper with the shorthand outline, and you are wasting the time of the student in a most reprehensible way. It is surely a golden rule in modern methods of teaching: "Never let your students do longhand into shorthand, but make them do plenty of spoken words into shorthand!" Even the Theory Certificate Tests should be from dictation rather than from the visual image, and this appreciation of a fundamental principle in the teaching of shorthand is a most important cause of success; training the ear embraces much more than this also. The large and important matter of aural comprehension is involved. How much of what they hear do your students fully understand? How well and for how long can they carry this understanding in their minds? Also involved is the ability to "carry" the spoken word mentally, so that anxiety does not interfere with performance when the student is writing a number of words behind the speaker. The physical power of hearing, the acuity of which varies quite dramatically among individuals, is another important factor.

Training the Fingers

The next skill to consider is the skill of the fingers. Here the value of copying correct shorthand falls naturally into place. It is again unnecessary to say that this copying should begin with the first lesson and be carried through right to the end. In the early stages it is plain, straightforward copying. You will see that your student has a pen with a suitable nib (it is most important that the nib should be right); that the position of the fingers, hand, arm and body are correct; that the outlines are written in a good style of shorthand writing, and that they are written as outlines and not as a series of joined strokes. Students must be encouraged to make their pens travel as quickly as the standard of neatness allows, and care should be taken to prevent them from "drawing" their strokes. An outline of three strokes should be one flowing stroke, and not stroke—pause—stroke—pause—stroke. More is said of this in Chapter XII.

Training the Eye

The third skill is the training of the eye in reading back. Here insistence that students should read correctly written shorthand and their own shorthand notes falls naturally into place, as does insistence that if at all possible every bit of shorthand written by the student should be read back.

There are four ways through which the reading or transcription may take place. The shorthand may be turned sometimes into thought words, sometimes into spoken words, sometimes into pen-and-ink *symbols*, and sometimes into typewritten *symbols*. (Note the important distinction between words and symbols.) Ideally in a commercial college it should be all spoken words at one end and typewritten symbols at the other. This would mean a very large extension of the typewriting sections in our colleges to enable each student to have, as well as his typewriting period, at least another period for the transcription of shorthand. This, of course, is a difficulty of expensive equipment.

In so far as it is impossible to transcribe everything on the typewriter, which of the other possibilities should be adopted for that remainder which cannot be done on the typewriter? Clearly, it should be a mixture of all three. Far too much longhand pen-work is done in our teaching. Generally speaking, except for test purposes, pen-and-ink transcription should never take place during the shorthand lesson, because to write longhand during the shorthand hour is a deplorable waste of shorthand-teaching time.

When we come to consider all three skills together, it is very fortunate that the development of any one of these three skills of widely separated human mechanisms helps the development of the others. That each skill helps the other is due to the fact that they all work in terms of the same shorthand outline, which is taken out of a common storehouse in the brain. Yet, while the development of each skill does help in the development of the others, a proper teaching of shorthand for practical purposes can come only from a proper balance of the three kinds of skill development. *None* of the three should be omitted. This is no idle point. It is possible for a student to know shorthand only through the skill of the eye in reading. Instances may be produced of those whose work lies in reading only; while they are highly skilled readers of shorthand, they are most inefficient both in the skill of writing from dictation and in the skill of outline formation at the pen point.

Skill Training

In skill training the same principles of teaching apply as in any other class of subjects, but in general the knowledge content of a skill is limited whilst the active content predominates. The things "to know" in shorthand are limited to the consonants, vowels, the alternative forms and when to use them, and those arbitraries which have been called grammalogues or short forms. The bulk of class work on the other hand is practice and repetition.

The requisite knowledge which must precede action is imparted in the same way as any other knowledge, but its use in practice and repetition follows one basic rule, namely, trial and satisfaction with the result, and this is based on interest, a condition far more important in skill learning than in book learning. Success in shorthand teaching is based on the feeling of progress that the pupil has at the end of each lesson (page 18). Indeed, one might crystallize the thought into two aphorisms: organize for success by obviating failure, and proceed through trial to success by obviating error.

A skilled movement can usually be broken down into its component parts, and the expert craftsman who is incapable of analysing his own movements cannot hope to become an expert teacher of his skill. He may, however, appreciate his own shortcomings and depend upon the slow-motion film to illustrate the component parts of what is to him a simple movement in itself. To deserve the title of a skilled person, a worker must exercise his calling with ease and precision and with smoothness and rhythm.

Ease can only come if posture is right, and if tools are good and handled correctly. Sitting at the desk, the position of the hands, the head and even the feet, and the avoidance of unnecessary muscular movement require attention. In shorthand teaching the tools are pen, ink and paper, and something will be said about pen (page 147) and paper (page 128) at a later stage.

Smoothness follows if freedom of motion is assured,

if from the beginning strokes and outlines are freely made, not carefully drawn but taught as handwriting is now often taught through a free arm movement.

The teaching of shorthand in so far as it can be taught as a skill has suffered from the analogy of teaching handwriting in the past. The old method of analysing letters into their component parts is now somewhat discredited, and words are considered as "wholes" and treated as such in the development of a cursive handwriting. In the same way in shorthand writing, an outline must be treated as a whole and not analysed into its component parts—and there must be a certain rhythm in its execution. Some teachers rather doubt the ability of children to achieve rapid writing of outlines in the early stages, but a speed of from 50 to 60 words per minute from the beginning is a reasonable aim.

Time and motion study in industry is really the application of the fundamental rule for skill learning to the many skills that go to make up a whole factory organization.

Method in skill training can be carried out either by demonstration of the movements of the skill, or by oral instruction. It is assumed that the teacher is a skilled craftsman, and, in the case of shorthand, blackboard demonstration and demonstration with pen and notebook are both of great importance. The student who can see a skilled movement taking place is desirous of emulating the method by which the movement is carried out. In the teaching of skills, the instinct of emulation can be used with advantage (page 29).

Similarly in the teaching of typewriting, the skilled operator with the ability of analysing the necessary movements is at a great advantage. Oral instruction should not, however, be wholly neglected, and the "telling" method, with demonstration, is important.

CHAPTER VII

MEMORY

We have already seen how ideas are taken into the mind through interest and retained only by association. Anything heard or seen and not apperceived fails to become a part of our mental make-up from which we can readily draw and cannot enter into our future conscious state, or, in plain language, cannot easily be remembered. This is the chief secret of memory, and it is on this basis that schools of mind-training flourish—on the practical application of the theories of education expounded by Herbart and based on apperception. We remember nothing without prompting; some cue is always to be found for the mental image that at any moment occupies our field of consciousness.

Habit and Memory Associated

The close relationship which exists between habit formation and memory is very real, and things are best remembered if they have been repeated, just as it is easier to do things when they have been done repeatedly. The same form of brain path is beaten out in both processes, because in both cases there have been an external stimulus and a nervous reaction, the only difference being that in the former case there may have been no actual muscular effort in the way of writing, walking, etc., although muscular effort of a vocal, visual or aural kind may have followed.

Native Retentivity

We must not assume that associations when once formed will remain permanently in the mind, otherwise a poem learnt as such, mainly by reasons of the association of the words in their context, would always be at command. We know, unfortunately, that even with the *cue* of a familiar extract, the remainder often escapes us. This is because two factors come into play: firstly, the mind, as a compartment in which our associated experiences are stored; and, secondly, our own facility for unlocking the store and producing the required experience. The first is a matter of gift, the second of education. We cannot alter the one; but as teachers it is our function to see that the storehouse is in an orderly condition, and that, however poor the store of experiences, they are to hand and can be reproduced to meet the various emergencies of life. Plainly put, we must accept the fact that some of our students are blessed with naturally retentive memories, whilst others are not equally endowed. Let us suppose that the brain of these two classes is differently constituted. Both may be equally plastic and receive impressions; but in the latter class it may be more elastic, and the impression will not be retained. If the difference is physiological, the native memory, that with which we are born, cannot be improved. Opinions differ in this matter and some psychologists believe that ability to recall can be improved. In any event, we can train our pupils to get the most out of what they have. This does not in any way imply that the person with a less retentive memory may not be as good a business man and citizen as the one who is better endowed in this respect. It does, however, mean that the teacher must take psycho-physiological facts into account, and remember that in this matter of memory the unit is the *individual* and not the class. Naturally, the good memory makes for economy in learning; but memory is only one faculty of mind, and in estimating mental worth consideration must be given to the natural impulses which may compensate.

Whole or Part

It may be useful to give some consideration to the question of the size of the project proposed for learning by rote and the possible relationship this has to acquiring or learning a skill. It is suggested that in learning poetry the "whole" method is superior to the "part" method, that is, the poem is best learned by reading it again and again as a whole rather than by taking it line by line. Modern evidence of the findings of psychological research indicates that for most people this is so. There is also the important consideration that grasping a whole enables us better to co-ordinate the parts within that whole and understand them. To put it a little more technically, the links of association are more securely welded. What is learned as a whole may also be learned more economically in time and effort. Still we are left with the decision what is a "whole," and what is a "part." Clearly one could not learn the whole theory of shorthand at a single application. An illustration may help. It may often be found useful to give intelligent students a conspectus of a whole—as, for example, the use of the *shun* hook, before going into more detail with each separate part. In this way, the relationship of and reasons for the different elements would become safely bound together as a whole in the mind. It is axiomatic that we remember only things we have learned and retained and are able to recall at pleasure. There is evidence that we can learn and retain without being able to recall without some effort, and this fact gives us two possibilities: (i) ability to recall, which we call good memory; and (ii) failure to recall, which is foregetting or bad memory. Ability to recall can be improved, and one of the means of improvement is association, the time or place of learning, the conditions under which we learned, and a host of other associated matters which may help us to recall what we have learned. Memory is as truly that with which we forget as it is that with which we remember, depending on ability to recall. We usually speak of "forgetting" as if it were reprehensible, but it may be of value that we can forget the unnecessary provided we retain and recall the essentials.

Bases of Memory

Let us see what the experimental psychologist has to say on the subject of memory. Experiments have been made (you can do them for yourselves, but it is not your job) in which a short list of words unrelated to each other, but having some interest to the students tested, is read aloud, the students being informed that they will be called upon to reproduce the words in the list, in any order, when the reading is over. In the reading one of the words is repeated three times. Results of the writing show that the majority of the class will remember the first word, the last word and the repeated word, and any word particularly interesting. Thus in a test taken just before a holiday period, the word "Easter," say, will have a particular interest. This is said to prove that the bases of recollection are—

the first word — primacy
the last word — recency
the repeated word — repetition
the interesting word — interest

These results do actually accord with our experience of life. "First impressions are lasting" is a familiar expression accepted by all. Paths most often used and most recently trodden are most likely to be trodden again, and thus repetition and recency are most likely to be real bases of recall. Finally, in actual life the incident that interests us, to which we give our attention, is the incident that is most easily recollected.

How is this to help us as teachers of shorthand?

Whole or Part in Shorthand Learning

We are aware that in shorthand learning certain facts must be learned by heart, as for example the consonants. Shall they be learned as a whole taking all the symbols used for the consonantal sounds as one dose, or shall they be learned in part as groups? The poetry analogy cannot be applied, as in shorthand the learning of facts has to be applied to the practice of a skill, that is the writing of shorthand. The balance of evidence in favour of the "whole" method does not necessarily apply in the teaching of a skill where the material learnt must be worked up into a finished product. Only gradually can the skill of knitting, carpentry or any muscular skill be acquired. In a lesser degree this applies to shorthand, and the method of presentation is at the choice of the teacher.

The extreme example of the whole and part method of learning when applied to shorthand is the reading approach in which *no writing* of shorthand is undertaken until the student is a fluent reader from printed shorthand (page 128). After this stage the student has another skill to master, namely, the *writing* of shorthand. It is submitted that the "part" system is preferable, the student learning to write at the same time as he learns to read.

Having accepted the principle that memory can be aided along the lines of primacy, recency, repetition and interest, let us again say that interest lies at the basis of all. The primary impression of the student of commercial subjects on entering the shorthand classroom for the first time will doubtless be a lasting impression, and it behoves the teacher to devote himself to the new student. The first impressions that our students get of us are important. Remember that they are as strangers in a strange land. Make them at home.

Adolescents are naturally shy creatures despite an apparent self-assurance. The creation of an impression of kindness and help outside your subject is an immeasurable memory aid which will bear fruit in the easier memorizing of short forms, and later in the mastery of exceptions to general rules which the student will meet in his speed-practice days.

Primary Impressions

At the first class meeting, clear the air of any idea that shorthand is difficult to learn. It is merely a matter of a new representation in which instead of P, p, *p*, *p*, 𝒫, 𝒫, we invariably use ╲ and similarly throughout. Show your students that in its most intricate moments it is simpler than many Eastern methods of writing taught as a matter of course to Eastern children. Take away that idea of mystery which some teachers delight in, and show the subject in the light of a simple cryptogram which can be read by *anyone* taking trouble. Commence your first lesson on the lines suggested, and the primary impression given will remain and, at the same time, will arouse interest in the next and each succeeding lesson.

The bases of recency and repetition can be combined. All repetition is a renewal and the making of a new recency. Therefore, let no lesson pass without a revision of old rules. Let your exercises *always* include examples of old principles already known, as well as examples illustrating the new rule. In a lesson on the alternative stroke and hook for *n* and their use in vowel indication, do not be afraid of harking back to similar use of stroke and circle *s* and of upward and downward *r*. Give your new matter a peg upon which to hang itself in the memory. This is what is meant by orderly grouping or creating of associations.

On the basis of what has been said it is well to remember that regular practice each day of the week is likely to be more beneficial than a weekly period of even more extensive practice.

Mnemonics Justified?

Here a word may be said about mnemonics, or the creation of artificial links of association. Is the use of the mnemonic a justifiable educational expedient? The answer is undoubtedly in the affirmative; but its use must be limited. Any mnemonic must be simple, direct, related to the subject-matter, and must act promptly as a cue. Years ago the writer was given the sentence—

Richard of York gained battles in vain.

as a means of remembering the order of the colours of the spectrum, namely, red, orange, yellow, green, blue, indigo, violet. The sentence stuck; but, like the knot tied on the handkerchief to aid memory, its relationship to the thing to remember was often hazy and fleeting. Often again the memory aid is clumsy and too elaborate to be justified. Shorthand teachers have several mnemonics which are quite good. The best of its kind is the double sentence for recalling the vowels and their order, but by the time this is useful it should be unnecessary—

Pa, may we all go too? and
That pen is not much good.

The *shun* mnemonic for the rules of *shun* following a

straight stroke is a fair one; but again let the students realize that it is only a device to aid memory. Let them understand why the rules are so framed. Be honest with them. Do not confuse them by talking about continuity of motion where none exists. Get them to see that the hook goes on the side opposite to the initial attachment, because of the danger of curving the straight stroke and so producing all the elements for misreading, namely, initial circle inside an apparent curve followed by *shun* inside the curve. A mnemonic is of value only if it acts readily as a cue to the proper understanding of the principle concerned.

Outlines are Based on Expediency

The writer has heard teachers dilate upon the merits of an outline. On one occasion the merits of the form in preference to the form was the subject of some minutes' talk, when, in reality, the occasion would have been better served by giving examples and obtaining the general rule by induction and by referring to expediency rather than to any rule as to so-called "continuity of motion" which, in this particular case, and many others, was probably never present in the mind of the inventor of the system. There is, however, a reason for every form and device adopted, and the search for *real* reasons repays as forming another association in the pupils' minds. It is good to learn a rule; it is even better to learn the reasons for it.

The secret of the mnemonic lies in the fact that isolated experiences independent of past experience cannot exist in the mind. The greater the number of past experiences to which a new experience can be related, the firmer will the new experience be fixed. Thus the relationship between—

race, *racy*; *loose*, *Lucy*;

fun, *funny*; *full*, *fully*;

vale, *valley*;

is better remembered than if one only of the pairs is referred to for an illustration of vowel indication. If we think of *loose* and *Lucy*, *fun* and *funny*, and then *vale* and *valley*, the outlines for *full* and *fully* rise automatically into view and are more ready to be recalled at need than before.

Thinking as a Memory Aid

Facts are fixed by the process of thinking. Get your students to think; lead them from cause to effect, and from effect to use; and facts will become part of the mental make-up. If a student makes his own rules, as has been previously suggested, and, before framing the rule in precise language, the teacher allows the student to use the rule by taking down dictation, memory is aided and the teacher is educating in the fullest sense. It is not so much the *matter* as the *method* that is educational. In Chapter IV we suggested that the cause of interest is *use*, and for this very reason interest is stronger than repetition as a basis of recollection. Nevertheless, repetition has been too much condemned, and, just as repetition is the foundation of habit or muscular memory, so must we find room for repetition or rote learning in shorthand teaching. The expression "learn by doing" is sound, as we saw in the previous chapter; but let us add a word of warning. Writing rules in longhand is entirely a waste of time. Writing is an automatic exercise, and many of us know that copying is too often done mechanically and without real attention to the sense of what is copied.

If the rule be in the textbook it is not necessarily made the student's own by letting him copy it into his notebook. The sounder plan is to let him use the textbook for extra-class reading or homework and to take plenty of dictation in class. *Reduce the writing of longhand to a minimum, except by way of transcription*, which is the practical end of most shorthand writing.

How are the associations on which learning is based, created? Summed up in a few words, we can say that they are created by thinking. This is the real essence of memory. Train your pupils to think for themselves. It is your province to direct their efforts, and the more they think for themselves, the better for you and them.

Interest and Memory

There is a peculiar fact about memory which has been overlooked. Up to the present we have been considering the native retentivity with which we are born. We have seen that it is possible that it cannot be improved, but that if used aright it will serve its purpose. Now, a person with little native retentivity may memorize and have at hand quite a stock of facts about a given subject; but he may not be able to remember facts about another subject entirely unrelated to his particular speciality. He may have studied history or chemistry by modern methods; or, again, he may be so interested in sport that he has at hand the record of the success or failure of his favourite team and its various opponents in the league matches over a succession of years; or, as a follower of the "sport of kings," he may know much about form and racing matters. All this arises from interest and association; but he might find difficulty in remembering matters in which he has little interest or which have no relation to his daily work. The man with no interest in bridge would not remember how the cards have run; but as a stock-broker he would tell how prices of various holdings in which he was interested have run during the day. Thus a graduate in Science or Arts may be unable to acquire the art of shorthand, or a knowledge of accounts, or the skill of typewriting, with greater rapidity than can the student direct from the secondary school. It is a commonplace to find such persons desiring to have an intensive course of what they call commercial training to fit them for a job in life as a secretary or the like. They certainly have the right attitude of mind and have grown accustomed to give voluntary attention; but they *must* go through the same processes as other students. Their previous education makes them more ready to meet the emergencies of their new study; but the same rule as to "cramming" applies. Dr. Franklin Jones says: "Cramming is attempted memory through repetition and recency; but the essential key, thinking, is lacking; and then the ideas loosely jumbled into mind soon fall out from the lack of connecting roots." The intensive course in this sense is a snare and a delusion, but in the sense of repetition and daily practice it is a sound idea.

Avoid Unimportant Exceptions

The reader must not think that by this we mean that much time was not formerly wasted in the teaching of purely formal subjects in the commercial-school curriculum. The fault has lain in method. In shorthand the teacher has endeavoured to impart everything he knows on every individual shorthand principle, and the student has been surfeited by rule and exception. The teacher of history, geography, mathematics, grammar and the rest would make no such attempt. The grammarian is content with a *few working facts* with the beginner in his subject, with copious examples to illustrate—and why not the teacher of shorthand with his? Such a plan demands that shorthand shall be considered as one subject and not two (theory and speed), and the slogan should be "speed (dictation) from the beginning and theory to the end." The teacher in the speed room must cease to be merely a reader, and must remain a teacher, constantly revising the theory systematically, renewing the students' acquaintance with rules, building up vocabulary as he goes along, and introducing the less common exceptions as they occur.

A Session's Work

With this method the evening-class teacher can accomplish in one winter session the real practical result of gaining speed-writing ability. The average student, if such there be, can attain a speed of from 50 to 60 words per minute on *new matter with a vocabulary within his educational range* in a session of twenty-six weeks, with classes held during three or four hours weekly, and two hours' weekly home exercises. This is not intensive training, but real educative work, depending on the broadness of outlook of the teacher and the flexibility of his methods of approach. As a textbook (for homework purposes) in such classes, the *New Course* or the *Modern Course* is to be recommended. (See pages 152–179.)

Shorthand, being a subject in which sensory-motor co-ordinations are brought into play, should be practised daily, like lacing the shoes, which by daily habit becomes automatic. On Sunday one may wear slip-on shoes without great injury to the habit.

CHAPTER VIII

MATTER

A SMALL book on the principles of teaching can only touch lightly on a consideration of the content of a syllabus, nor is it necessary to consider the extent of the details with which a shorthand teacher is called upon to deal. A consideration of the order of presentation and the medium through which the matter is presented is, however, worthwhile.

The aim of the shorthand teacher is to train students to be able to record the spoken word, and usually thereafter to produce a perfect transcript. It is well known that Pitman's shorthand is capable of use for the taking down of dictation at speeds beyond ordinary normal human utterance, but for practical purposes the average business student is satisfied with a speed of from 120 to 140 words per minute. It is worthwhile considering how this speed can be attained.

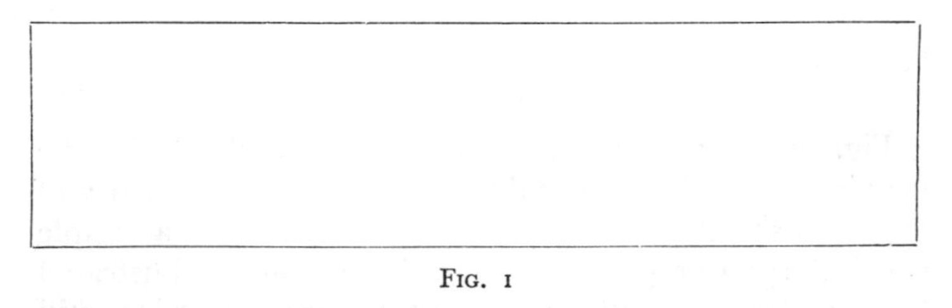

FIG. 1

Fig. 1 represents the teaching required to bring a student to 120 words per minute. This teaching can be applied vertically or horizontally until the space is filled.

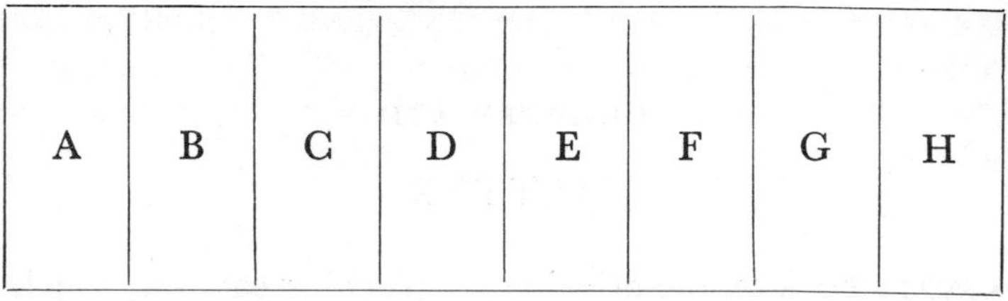

A	B	C	D	E	F	G	H

Fig. 2

Fig. 2 represents the same material divided into sections, Section A representing for example all that will ever be taught in relation to consonants and vowels; B all that need be taught regarding circle *s*, *stee* and *ster* loops and the *sway* circle; C the initial and final hooks; D the halving and doubling principles; E alternative forms of all kinds—contractions, prefixes, suffixes, intersections, etc.; and F, G and H the progressive steps in speed practice, finally reaching 120 words per minute.

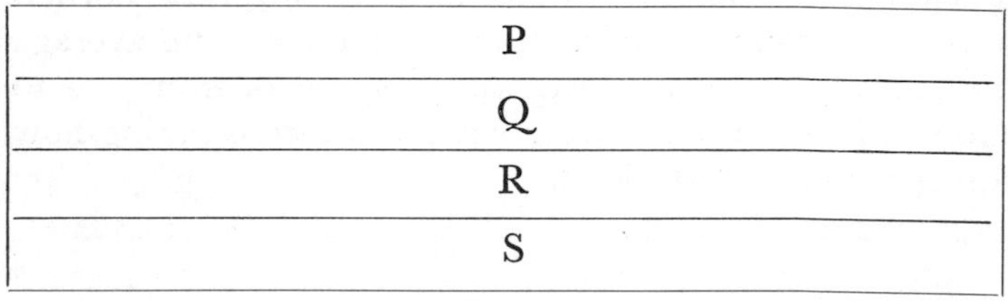

P
Q
R
S

Fig. 3

Fig. 3 represents the same final result with the training applied horizontally. P represents the theory of Pitman's shorthand as illustrated by means of a simple vocabulary; Q represents the additional theory illustrated by a wider vocabulary; R and S speed practice, still enlarging vocabulary.

These diagrams are intended to illustrate the fact that, as in all other subjects in the school curriculum, different methods of approach may be used in order to attain the same final result. If the time taken to achieve these results is the same independently of the order in which the material is presented, the choice is immaterial and is dependent upon the wishes and plans of the individual teacher.

It is submitted that, particularly in schools where the weekly allocation of time to shorthand is not very generous, there is a distinct advantage in the horizontal idea, as it gives at an early stage a feeling of mastery and ability to put the subject of shorthand to practical use.

Assuming that in *x* hours a given class of students can cover A, B and part of C in Fig. 2, and that in the same time another class covers P in Fig. 3, which set of students is the better equipped? Clearly the latter. Class 1 will be unable to use their shorthand, except for selected exercises. Many simple words come under the principles to be dealt with in the rest of C and in D and E (Fig. 2), whereas all the principles have been touched upon by Class 2, and the intelligent student by analogy or application is in a position to write numerous words not perhaps already dealt with—at any rate a member of Class 2 has an equipment which as it stands is useful, and which encourages him to return for more.

The principles of Pitman's shorthand are often exemplified by means of words and exercises which are not always within the mental attainment of the shorthand pupil, particularly in our junior evening institutes. In consequence the enthusiastic teacher must of necessity teach more than shorthand in the very limited time allotted to him for his work. No teacher worth his salt will object to filling in gaps in the English education of his students in their own language, but the allocation of time is all too short, and only a small proportion of it can be spared in the initial stages for vocabulary building.

In any subject of the curriculum it is usual to carry out the teaching in a vocabulary which is understood by the students concerned, and this should apply equally with shorthand. Not only are we too prone to exemplify our rules by using words beyond the capacity of some of our pupils, but we are much too ready to talk like text-books about "vowel indication" for instance—an excellent phrase amongst teachers, but hardly appreciated at its proper worth by the tired adolescent. "Vowel indication" and "medial use" of shorthand devices are things to be practised and not talked about: or at least in a way that will make them come alive to the student.

In this question of English material for shorthand teaching we are handicapped by the make-up of our classes. It is one thing to say teach a subject within the vocabulary familiar to the student, and quite another to gauge the vocabulary which is a common denominator in the class. The expert teacher will always ensure that in choice of words he is not above the level of his class, and where necessity arises he will see to it that his students are made acquainted with the meaning and use of words and phrases which he must introduce at a given stage. Every teacher of shorthand can, however, obtain assistance in this question of vocabulary by adopting what may be considered the mean vocabulary of his class—a vocabulary that represents a high percentage of the words in everyday use. It may be suggested that words in common use vary according to environment, and this is true, but it is not a constructive criticism because from the shorthand point of view facility in writing words in common use is the backbone of shorthand success. Ten short forms in Pitman's shorthand make up 25 per cent of any continuous English matter, and if to these we add just under 700 of the commonest words in the language, arrived at on a careful count of the words used by many persons in many circumstances in life, we have (counting their derivatives) covered about 80 per cent of words as they appear in continuous English. If for want of an exact knowledge of the available vocabulary of each unit in the class we accept a "word count" vocabulary, we are at any rate making an attempt at simplification.

The charge may be levelled that we are treating the theory of shorthand with scant ceremony, but this is not the case. Sound theory is essential to good shorthand, and the amount of training in theory required in any method of presentation cannot be cut down. The danger is that the reader may misunderstand the aim—it is "dictation from the beginning and theory to the end." Thoroughness is essential, and when the stage of dictation approaches the rate of normal speech the teacher must continue to revise and expound the theory and exemplify with a wider vocabulary.

The question of the student's vocabulary is not the only element in favour of the teaching of preliminary theory through a selected vocabulary. There is another practical and logical reason that may be advanced in favour of this basis. Shorthand is written at speed out of the store of outlines known and at the pen point of the writer, and to only a minute degree out of the ability to apply theoretical knowledge to new words. The greater the store of pen-point outlines, the greater the facility, and with a selected vocabulary and *much repetition* a plentiful supply of known outlines is secured—"known," that is, to the extent of what psychologists call overlearning, the point where the response arises from the stimulus without conscious thought or effort. Sir James Pitman has made a selection of some 700 words for *preliminary* theory teaching, and these comprise about 68 per cent of the words used by the average educated man. With their derivatives they amount to as much as 80 per cent. These, by constant repetition, and drill, give an automatic pen-point ability which will form the basis of great facility when the vocabulary is properly built up in the speed stages of training.

The organization of large schools, the periodic tests, and the aim in their compilation may be stumbling-blocks in the way of change in method of presentation. The difficulty is that shorthand has been looked upon as two subjects—theory and speed—and these subjects have been subdivided into elementary and advanced theory and into different styles. The truth is that there is one subject—"Shorthand"—and there is no such thing as elementary and advanced except as convenient divisions, any more than there is elementary and advanced hand-writing. Where, however, this subdivision exists, based on one or other of the textbooks or on the requirements of the school organization, a variation in mode of presentation can be successful only where the staff works as a team and the individual members of the staff know and accept the conditions.

Theory tests should be based on the words with which the students have had the opportunity to become familiar and on the continuous context of sentences. A true test of progress at any stage during the learning process ought to incorporate not only dictation within the vocabulary taught, but the ability to read shorthand, and transcribe it under some pressure of time, to vocalize outlines, and to write with an acceptably accurate and properly formed penmanship.

We cannot do better in dealing with "word frequency" than, in the next chapter, to produce the views of Sir James Pitman on this subject.

CHAPTER IX

WORD FREQUENCY

A GREAT deal of research work has been done on the question of the frequency with which words recur in written English and it is undoubtedly true that benefit to the teaching of English, particularly in the form of shorthand, can be obtained by a wise use of the data available. All teachers of shorthand can benefit by adapting their teaching methods to takc into account this important principle. Teachers in evening classes, and in some day schools usually get so small an allocation of time for shorthand that daily practice cannot be given to the degree desirable, and accordingly for them an approach to the subject which takes into account word frequency is almost essential, since it is all the more important that the time available for practice should be directed to the best possible advantage. Even teachers in those day schools which are able to give a regular time each day to the teaching of shorthand cannot afford to overlook the possibility of wise drilling which takes into account this factor in shorthand teaching.

What is Frequency?

If, then, the teacher agrees that the principle of word frequency has a bearing on his teaching, he may well ask for guidance—at what stage, for instance, is a word so frequent that it is especially important and worth repeating in daily practice? This chapter sets out to give the teacher an answer to this question, and to give guidance, so that the teacher may select and present as teaching material just those words which are important.

Teachers will no doubt want to know and to understand up to what stage the principle of word frequency is important, and to be given guidance in the application of the principle. The most satisfactory publication covering the really common words is considered to be *Relativ Frequency of English Speech Sounds*, by Dewey (Sir Isaac Pitman & Sons Ltd.). This book gives a list of 1,027 words which recurred at least 11 times in the course of 100,000 words. For example, at one end of the list the word "the" recurred 7,310 times, while at the other end the word "worse" recurred 11 times. It also gives a list showing the number of times each of 1,131 words, including any derivatives which recurred 11 times or more frequently, did in fact recur.

500 Words the Optimum

Clearly this is a most useful book for the shorthand teacher, for it gives with exactitude the ascertained order of frequency of all the common English words. But, the teacher will ask, where is the line to be drawn at which frequency may be said to be of sufficient importance to influence shorthand teaching? After consideration and the preparation of a graph showing the curve of the falling off of frequency, it was decided (admittedly as an act of judgment) that the line should be drawn somewhere between the 400 and 500 mark, and that 500 should be taken as the dividing line. It is most fortunate that this figure, chosen as a round figure, should have provided not only the means of explanation of the reasons for the judgment, but a complete confirmation of that judgment.

The 501st word in the list mentioned above is the word "patriot." The reader will almost certainly—and it is thought rightly—exclaim that this particular word is not to be regarded as a frequently occurring word, and is not one which should merit special treatment in the routine of teaching shorthand. However, there is another consideration which is equally unexpected. The word "saucer" is not even in the 10,000 commonest words of the Horn List (this figure is 10,000, and not a mistake for 1,000), yet the word "saucer" will be considered by the teacher to be not only a reasonably common word, but one within the vocabulary of even quite small infants.

What is the explanation of this apparently contradictory evidence? The answer is clearly that only up to a limit of frequency (apparently to be drawn somewhere below 501) does the pattern of the English language produce recurrence of words irrespective of the subject which is dealt with. The words "the," "of," "and," "that," etc., recur very frequently because of the pattern of the English language, and not because of the subject-matter or because of the habits of English of the writer.

On the other hand, words of such a frequency that they come outside the first 500 are more influenced by the subject-matter and the habits of English of the writer (or dictator) than by the pattern of the language. For example, the Dewey list in question was prepared as to 30 to 60 per cent from newspaper and magazine articles, speeches and editorials, matter which might be thought to have been influenced by the War or other considerations likely to bring in the words "patriot," "patriotism," "patriotic," "unpatriotic," and the other derivatives of this word. It would no doubt be as true to say that the word "patriot" happens to occur as No. 501 because of the accident of the choice of material, as that the word "saucer" might easily have appeared as No. 501 if the material chosen as a sample had happened to be business correspondence taken from the office of a firm selling household china, or had contained Hans Andersen's famous fairy story about the "dog with eyes as large as saucers." Clearly, the shorthand teacher (who cannot predict the type of special business vocabulary which individual students will require, any more than he can predict the special words which will be contained in the next examination test material) is especially interested only in those words which the business man, the examiner, and in fact all those who use English must use, and must of necessity keep on using.

The first 500 words in the list occurred (with their derivatives) 76,611 times; the second 500 occurred only 9,250 times. The 500th word occurred 27 times; the 1,000th word occurred 12 times. These facts are clearly so significant as to confirm the more theoretical argument centred on the words "patriot" and "saucer," and to justify, as far as justification can be given, the statement that for shorthand purposes the factor of frequency is predominantly important only up to the first 500 common words, and that words from 500 upwards if important to the shorthand writer and teacher are important only because of considerations other than mere frequency.

Considerations Other than Frequency

It is a fact that there are to the shorthand teacher and writer reasons other than frequency for the teaching of a word that lies outside the 500 commonest words. An arbitrary figure of 200 words was added to make the round figure of 700, to supply the teacher with those words which it was considered might be most useful for shorthand purposes. Examples will be given showing that there are words which are important to the shorthand writer and teacher for reasons other than mere frequency. For instance, the word "mother" contains a meaning which is frequently wanted, and for which there is no alternative by a combination of common words. In contra-distinction, the word "plain," although it is a comparatively common word, cannot be regarded as as important as "mother," since its meaning may be conveyed by the use of the more common words "clear" or "not beautiful," all of which are words in this selected list.

Frequency and Meaning

Words are therefore introduced in the balance of 200 which are of value because they combine a frequency factor with a factor of conveying meaning. This factor of conveyance of meaning is an important one in practice, since it is the factor which enables interesting connected matter to be written within the extraordinary restrictive conditions imposed by the self-limitation of using only 700 words. In fact, it can be safely assumed that readers who turn to the shorthand or the printed English in the *700 Common-word Reading and Dictation Exercises* will be surprised to be told that the vocabulary is limited to 700 words and selected derivatives.

Frequency and Provision of Examples

Just as the capacity for conveying meaning, when combined with a factor of frequency, is important, so, too, to the shorthand teacher is the factor of provision of examples in the important principles of the system. If, as is the case, the word "instructions" has a reasonably high factor of frequency and is wanted as an example of the use of the *instr*-loop (a shorthand device), it should be considered as having a strong claim for inclusion in the extended list. Clearly, therefore, if there occurs in conjunction a factor of frequency combined with a factor of shorthand-teaching utility, such a word should be added to the list. Similarly, special outlines and short forms which it is desired that the student should learn by rote have been included. Examples of these are (i) "perhaps" and (ii) "immediately." These are not in the first 500 common words, and are not wanted for their meaning, since a variation of the words (i) "maybe" and (ii) "quickly" is always appropriate. On the other hand, the teacher intends the student to learn these words, and wants him to learn them largely by rote, and therefore their inclusion within a list of words to be used for repetitive drill purposes is clearly desirable.

The Justification for Derivatives

There remains only the justification for the inclusion of derivatives. The principle of word-building is such an important and well-known principle of the teaching of Pitman's shorthand that it was thought that, when once the student had learnt circle *s*, it would be artificial to treat "makes" as a different word from "make." Similarly, when the student knew the *st* loop, it would be wrong to treat the past participle "faced" as anything but a basic variation of the present tense "face." A careful selection has therefore taken place in the preparation of the derivatives, and only those words are included which lend themselves to building from the root word, using the main principles of Pitman's shorthand.

It is believed that, as a result of this careful selection of the available research matter, this list represents the ideal combination between the two factors of frequency and the limitation of vocabulary for the purpose of teaching any repetitive skill connected with the English language (and typewriting is here included as well as shorthand), and in particular for the teaching of Pitman's shorthand.

It is interesting to know that, notwithstanding the limitation to only 700, the words used in this list have a total frequency calculated from the tables of 68 per cent of all normal English for the root words and approximately 80 per cent for those words when their derivatives are included.

The Value of a Small Total

The important advantages for drill purposes of keeping down the number of words should not be overlooked by the teacher, who will be the first to appreciate the fact that if the purpose of the selection is to give repetitive practice and teach outlines by rote (even if they are originally learnt by a conscious application of rules) it is clearly desirable to keep the number of words down to such a figure as will ensure constant reiteration and set the minimum requirements of absorption into the memory. It is always more than proportionately easier for the student learning poetry by heart to become word perfect in ten lines than in a hundred. Similarly the student in learning a number of outlines comes to the stage of instant response very much more easily as the number is kept down.

Writing by Rote

This question of writing by memory or by rote should not be misunderstood. It will appear on consideration that the ultimate object of a shorthand teacher is to train students so that they can "see outlines in the air"—they must be able to visualize a shorthand outline for a word at least as quickly as they can visualize longhand. This capacity for instantaneous visualization, both in longhand and shorthand, passes by practice from the initial stage of laborious conscious effort in the application of what has been taught, to unconscious and instantaneous visualization and representation on the line of writing.

There is nothing wrong in saying that our students have to learn to write by rote. It would be a false view to think that a competent shorthand writer in writing the word "make" says to himself: "*m*, *kay*, *second position*, *omit the vowel*." There is no thinking at all, because the word "make" is part of his mental outfit, having been written many, many times and learnt by rote; it goes immediately on to paper as a copy of a mental image formed instantaneously.

If and when the writer hears the word "Elvetham," he visualizes an outline by the application of rules that he has learned from the background of words which he has already written, and, since such a word is not so immediately visualized, his response is not quite so instantaneous. The teacher cannot expect to teach all words that the student may at any future time be required to write, and he may safely agree that one of his important functions is to concentrate on the more common words so that there is produced in the student instantaneous visualization and representation.

The teacher is advised to use this selection of words first for reading practice. Let every student in the class read and re-read the outlines until the speed of reading is without hesitation, i.e., say, 140 words per minute. Then let the students have sufficient practice in copying until the teacher is confident that each student is able to reproduce every outline in a good style of penmanship, and without hesitation, i.e., the outline being written as a whole, and not as a series of joined strokes. Then let the teacher give plenty of dictation practice, repeating the same passage so that the speed is raised to 160 words per minute. The words should be preferably in continuous English, as, for instance, in the *700 Common-word Reading and Dictation Exercises.*

It should be borne in mind that the words selected are the common words of the language, and a student who can read pages based on them without hesitation, or write the shorthand outlines as a whole without hesitation is thereby capable of writing these words at 120 words per minute or more, because the signs of Pitman's shorthand are so simple and so quickly written that to maintain this speed is well within the capacity of any student who knows what he intends to write.

In the meantime there are two practical demonstrations which establish the value of the selection: (i) representative passages of standard English when analysed are found to contain overwhelming practical proof of the principle; (ii) passages written solely in the vocabulary demonstrate that the list is capable of giving interesting and varied matter in which the limitation and repetition are scarcely detectable.

PITMAN LIST OF COMMON WORDS

a
an
able
about
above
according
account
across
act
add
advantage
advertise
advertised
advertisement
after
afternoon
again
age
ago
agree
air
heir
all
along
also
altogether
am
among
amount
and
animal
announce
another
answer
any
in
appear
April
are
arm
army
art
as
has
ask
at
attempt
attention
August
authority
away
awe (See *ought*)
ay (See *I*)
baby
back
bad
balance
bank
base
be
beautiful
because
become
bed
before
begin
behind
belief
believe
believed
best
better
between
beyond
big
black
blue
board
body
book
both
bought
boy
buoy
brake (See *break*)
bread
break
brake
bring
brother
brought
build
building
built
buoy (See *boy*)
burn
business
but
buy
by
bye
call
came
can
capital
car
care
carry
case
cause
cell (See *sell*)
certain
change
character

charge
cheap
check
cheque
chief
child
children
city
clean
clear
coal
coarse (See *course*)
cold
colour
come
comfort
commit
common
company
competition
complete
condition
connect
consider
continue
control
copy
cost
could
country
course
coarse
cover
credit
cry
custom
cut
danger
date
day
dear
December
deep
degree
deliver
delivered
delivery
demand
depend
desire
detail
develop
die
dye
differ
difference
different
difficult
difficulty
direct
discover
distance
distribute
division
do
door
doubt
down
dress
drink
drive
during
dye (See *die*)
each
early
earth
ease
east
education
effect
either
electric
electricity
employ
end
engine
engineer
English
enough
equal
equally
even
event
ever
every
example
except
exchange
exchanged
exist
expect
expected
experience
expert
express
eye (See *I*)
face
fact
fall
family
far
farm
father
fear
February
feel
few
field
figure
final
find
fire
first

fish
fly
follow
food
foot
for
force
form
forward
free
frequent
Friday
friend
from
front
full
fully
further
future
gave
general }
generally }
gentlemen
get
girl
give }
given }
go
gold
good
govern }
governed }
government
great
ground
grow
had
half
hand
happen
happy
hard
has (See *as*)
have
he
head
health
hear }
here }
heart
heat
heavy
heir (See *air*)
help
her
here (See *hear*)
high
him
himself
his (See *is*)
history
hold
hole (See *whole*)
home
hope
horse
hour (See *our*)
house
how
however
hundred
I }
eye }
ay }
idea
if
immediate
important }
importance }
impossible
improve }
improved }
improvement }
in (See *any*)
increase
indeed
industry
influence
inform }
informed }
information
instruction
insurance
interest
iron
is }
his }
issue
it
itself
January
judge
July
June
just
keep
kind
king
knew (See *new*)
know (See *no*)
knowledge
labour
land
language }
owing }
large
last
late
law
lead

learn
least
leave
left
less
let
letter
life
light
like
limit
line
list
little
live
long
longer
look
loss
love
low
machine
made }
maid }
make
man
manufacture }
manufactured }
many
March
mark
market
marry
mass
master
matter
may
me
meal
mean
measure

meat }
meet }
member (See *remember*)
memory
mere }
Mr. }
method
might
mile
milk
million
mind
mine
minute
miss
modern
moment
Monday
money
month
more }
remark }
remarked }
morning
most
mother
motor
move
Mr. (See *mere*)
much
must
my
myself
name
nation
nature
near
necessary
need
neither

never }
November }
new }
knew }
news
next
night
no }
know }
nor
north
not
note
nothing
November (See *never*)
now
number }
numbered }
object }
objected }
observation
October
of
off
offer
office
official
often
oh! }
owe }
oil
old
on
once
one
only
open
operate
opinion
opportunity

or
order
organize }
organized }
organization
other
ought }
awe }
our }
hour }
ourselves
out
over
owe (See *oh!*)
owing (See *language*)
own
page
paint
paper
part
particular
party
pass
pay
peace }
piece }
penny
people
perfect
perhaps
person
personal
picture
piece (See *peace*)
place
plain }
plane }
plan
plane (See *plain*)
plant
play
please
pleasure
point
political
poor
position
possible
pound
power
present
price
principal }
principally }
principle }
probable }
probably }
probability }
product
profit
property
provide
public }
publish }
published }
pull
purpose
put
quality
quarter
question
quick
quite
rail
rate
rather }
writer }
reach
read
ready
real
really
reason
receive
recent
record
red
regard
regret
regular
relate
remark } (See *more*)
remarked }
remember }
remembered }
member }
report
represent }
represented }
require
respect }
respected }
responsible }
responsibility }
rest }
wrest }
result
return
right }
write }
river
road
room
round
rule
run
safe
said
sail }
sale }
same
satisfactory

Saturday
save
say
scene (See *seen*)
school
science
sea (See *see*)
second
see }
sea }
seem
seen }
scene }
self
sell }
cell }
send
sense
sent
September
serious
serve
service
set
several
sew (See *so*)
shall
she
shilling
ship
short
should
show
side
sign
simple
since
sir
sit
situation
six

size
small
so }
sew }
sow }
some }
sum }
sometimes
soon
sort
sound
south
sow (See *so*)
speak
special }
specially }
spend }
spent }
stand
start
state
station
steel }
steal }
step
still
stone
stop
store
story
straight
strange
street
strong
subject }
subjected }
success
such
suggest
sum (See *some*)
summer

Sunday
supply
support
sure
surprise
sweet
system
table
take
talk
tax
teach
tell
test
than
thank }
thanked }
that
the
their }
there }
them
themselves
then
there (See *their*)
therefore
these
they
thing
think
third
this
those
though
thought
thousand
through
Thursday
till
time
to

together
told
to-morrow
too }
two }
touch
toward }
trade }
town
trade (See *toward*)
train
tried
trouble
true
trust
truth
try
Tuesday
turn
two (See *too*)
under
until
up
upon
us
use
usual }
usually }
value
very
view
voice
waist (See *waste*)
walk
want
war
warm
was
waste }
waist }
watch
water
way (See *weigh*)
we
weak (See *week*)
weather
Wednesday
week }
weak }
weigh }
way }
well
went
were
west
what
whatever
when
whenever
where
whether
which
while
white
who
whole }
hole }
whom
whose
why
wide
will
window
winter
wire
wise
wish
with
within
without
woman
women
wonderful }
wonderfully }
word
work
world
worth
would
wrest (See *rest*)
write (See *right*)
writer (See *rather*)
writing
written
wrong
yard
year
yes
yesterday
yet
you
young
your

CHAPTER X

METHOD

We hear much about "method" and "methods of teaching" in these days, and there is a tendency to speak as if methods were something apart from subject-matter. In reality, *method* is merely *the way in which* the outside world or *impersonal experience* becomes a part of the student, that is, becomes *personal experience*. It is the "how" of teaching, and it cannot be divorced from the matter or "what" of teaching.

A doctor would not attempt to cure a sick person before diagnosing his complaint, and a teacher must not choose his method without reference to the matter taught. It is reasonable to state that the manner of teaching "how to do" cannot be decided without considering what is to be done. Some of the basic principles of method are now briefly described, showing how they may be utilized by the shorthand teacher.

Various Methods

The simplest way to approach this matter is to name in simple language the more important methods and, after a brief description, select those that are useful to us, and illustrate their use in relation to shorthand.

Here then are the methods: the objective method, the method of illustration, the laboratory or research method, the method of reasoning, and the telling method (including the textbook method); and, combined with any of these, the memory method.

Objective

The objective method is the only method suitable to very young pupils. All the primary ideas of childhood are gained from a knowledge of objects obtained through the senses. Touching, handling, smelling, tasting and seeing the actual thing means something to the child; his ideas of hardness, smoothness, softness, roughness, colour and form are wisely given through the objective method. The difficulty of conveying correct ideas of time and space exists only because these ideas cannot be taught objectively. *Teaching is objective when actual objects are used to deduce facts.*

Illustrative

Suppose facts are taught and then objects are furnished by way of illustration, or, if objects are not available and pictures or diagrams are used, the method becomes the method of illustration. In teaching the mechanism of the typewriter, both these methods are useful and a combination of them is excellent. A class lesson with a large diagram of the keyboard showing the "home keys" and the division of the keyboard provides an example of the illustrative method; whilst a lesson on the "scale," in which each student is expected to discover the principles underlying its use, is a natural development of the objective method in which apparatus is manipulated. This is the laboratory or research method of teaching. It holds an important place in education and, whilst it cannot be directly utilized in the teaching of shorthand, it must not be overlooked, for naturally it in turn develops into the method of reasoning.

Reasoning

In the process of building up the intellectual side of human beings, the order in which intellectual ability grows is from ideas to thoughts, and from thoughts to reasoning. Thus the smallest child can realize the forms but to him they are strokes or lines, mere ideas. Older people realize that, in Pitman's shorthand, they stand for sounds, and knowledge of this fact is due to thinking, which is nothing more than the process of putting together ideas. The production of correct thinking is the aim of all teaching. The next step, reasoning, is the examination of thoughts and the drawing of conclusions. This is the step which is useful to the shorthand teacher. We shall have more to say on the question when we examine the telling method, which is closely allied to what is still not unknown in teaching, namely, the textbook method, a variant of the telling method. The textbook is an adjunct to teaching, and not a substitute. For actual class work, put aside the textbook and, whilst using it in its proper place, boldly depart from its order and thereby you can sustain interest. Let your presentation be new and fresh. Do not be afraid of the unknown.

Induction

If a teacher writes the following outlines on the board, before the student has learnt the use of the circle and the hook as abbreviating devices, he arouses curiosity and hence interest—

pay, pray, pry, pain, spray, sprain, Spee,

sweep, Spain

He can elicit from his class that the common sound in the words is the sound of *p*, and the common element in the outlines is \ He can also obtain the information that the dot in the middle place evidently indicates *ā*.

Gradually, by this process, the three vowel places can be discovered and will be remembered. The rules can be given afterwards in a concise form; but the pupil will feel that they are *his* rules and not those of the book.

Next, the corresponding heavy sound *b* may be introduced, and an appropriate representation by means of a heavy stroke suggested. Immediately dictate—

bay, *Bray*, *brain*, *bane*, *brine*, *been*

The class has not yet formally learnt the *r* and *n* hooks, nor the diphthong; but what matter, if they learn informally, provided that the loose ends are gathered together later? You have a foundation upon which to build your future lesson on the hooks, initial and final. The idea is given and the new matter is easily associated with the old. Similarly, the circles and loops can be introduced incidentally, without spoiling the sequence of your textbook exercises.

What has been given so far in the discussion of this inductive process may be considered overmuch for any class except an intelligent group of post-G.C.E. grammar-school students. Its application could, of course, be quite easily restricted to only one or two elements at the same time, e.g. the vowel *ā*, the *pr* hook.

This method does not dispense with the necessity of the student diligently familiarizing himself with the whole of the shorthand alphabet, and remembering that there is no easy road to acquiring fundamental signs and symbols in any branch of learning.

If a pupil meets with many outlines containing, say, the form ⌒ and finds that each represents a number of sounds having a common element *em*, he immediately assumes that the shorthand sign for the sound *em* is ⌒ He reaches this assumption by the method of reasoning. Reasoning is of two kinds, namely, inductive and deductive. The method adopted of discovering the common element in the outlines shown above is the method of induction, and it is a very valuable aid to the teacher of shorthand.

Slow but Sure

The inductive method has the demerit that it is slower than the telling method mentioned later; but it is, nevertheless, very useful in the early stages. There is a more lasting effect in telling the significance of the following forms—

and then, by induction, obtaining the rules as to position of vowels and of outline, than in telling the position of the vowels and afterwards exemplifying to illustrate the rules.

In inductive teaching, the teacher should state the aim, so that the class may have the problem before it. A review of the previous lesson is sufficient for this, that is, the class must be prepared for the lesson, the material must be presented, conclusions or generalizations can be drawn, and the generalizations applied. The order of inductive teaching is: (i) presentation of a number of individual cases; (ii) generalization, or the discovery of rules and principles; and, finally, (iii) the application of such rules and principles. The important feature of the first step is the selection of appropriate and *sufficient examples*, as no generalization can be made on isolated facts.

The inductive method should not be attempted merely for the sake of logic or psychology; but all principles and rules which can be obtained in this way should be taught by this method, if time allows. The method has the great advantage that what is learned in this way is longer recalled and more readily applied. The student has made a mental effort which pays the dividend of more securely based learning.

Deduction

Deduction, the second form of reasoning, is informally utilized in all teaching. It consists of applying general notions to specific cases. A simple example of deductive reasoning, given merely as an example, is seen in the following—

Problem. How do we read the outline ? ?

First Statement. All initial attachments, save the initial hooks, are read before the strokes to which they are attached.

Second Statement. The large circle *sway* is an initial attachment; and

Conclusion. *Sway* is read before the stroke (and the outline represents *swim*).

The first statement is the generalization, and the second, or minor, statement is the one to which the general statement is to be applied. The common factor is the initial attachment, and the conclusion is drawn by combining the two statements.

Alliance of Induction and Deduction

Induction and deduction are closely allied. The first is said to proceed from individual to general, and the second from general to individual; but do not let the young teacher hesitate over names or over statements of their meaning; but let him get the notions of induction and deduction in his mind. Let him then proceed from rule to example, or from example to rule, as best fits the occasion. In actual practice the two methods are used side by side. Reasoning in daily life is neither wholly inductive nor wholly deductive.

The Telling Method

Many inexperienced teachers adhere wholly to the telling method. This is true not only of teachers of shorthand, but of teachers of history, literature and other humanistic studies.

To some extent the teacher of shorthand is right in his method; but variety in approach has the effect of securing and maintaining interest; and, as we have already seen, interest and attention are the mainsprings of education. Signs and symbols cannot in general be taught by any method of reasoning, but must be told or presented as facts; but the relation of the shorthand characters to the pupil's past experience, that is, to the familiar sounds of language, can be reasoned. If the teacher attempts this as he should, he will do it through induction and deduction.

The telling method, exemplified by what the writer would call the textbook method, is the easiest and most rapid method of teaching; but it is dangerous, since it is not to be relied upon. Even when accompanied by clever questioning, of which something will be said at a later stage, this method does not appeal to every pupil. There is the danger that the facts told or read convey little to the hearer, as he may not have in his stock of experiences associated ideas to which he can connect new matter. He has nothing with which to form an apperception. We have already seen that memory is a matter largely of linking up the old with the new.

Telling is Essential

In spite of this, the telling method is essential; and the teacher is the only one to decide under all the conditions of his teaching what he must tell and what must be developed by reason.

The Lecture

The greatest danger of the telling method is that it may deteriorate into the lecture, which is out of place in shorthand teaching, particularly for younger pupils. Indeed, the lecture in all school work is likely to become more and more discredited. The work of learning is the pupils' and that of lecturing is the teacher's. No effort is required on the pupils' part, and, as interest is not usually sustained where curiosity is not aroused, the lecture may fail in its object.

It is all too easy to discourse at length so that a "lesson" becomes all "chalk and talk." The temptation must be resisted. The "telling" element must be kept to an absolute minimum. Thereafter, the teacher must consolidate by questioning, by recapitulation with a different approach, and by practice.

The secret of successful telling in shorthand teaching is to tell a little at a time and to let the pupils do much. In an hour's lesson only a small fraction of the time should be devoted to instruction and questioning. The aim is to represent sound by symbol with readiness, and readiness can be achieved only by practice.

The Memory

The function of the mind which we call memory has

already been discussed, and the principles underlying the process of memorization are already familiar to the reader. Perhaps, however, we did not bring out with sufficient strength the dominant factor of interest. Interest is greatest when the new is combined with the old, and in doing this the teacher is repeating. Thus, in the revision of the old rules, we have *repetition*; the old rules themselves illustrate the further psychological basis of recall, *primacy*, whilst the new rules associated with the old exemplify *recency*. *Interest* aroused in this manner combines within itself primacy, repetition and recency.

With older students the use of the circles and loops may well be taught together, since the fundamental principle is the same; but, with a class of younger people where the small circle has been considered, the large initial circle and the *st* loop should be taught along with a revision of the rules for the use of the small circle initially. Again, in giving exercises for dictation, the wise teacher will go back for examples, linking up the new subject-matter with the old at every step, thus—

Sir, *star*, *sorry*, *starry*, *soup*, *stoop*, *swoop*, *stirrup*, *syrup*, *save*, *stave*, *Sam*, *stem*, *swim*.

Similarly, in a lesson on initial and final hooks, the exercise should not deal exclusively with the subject of the lesson, but should revise old rules and establish relations, thus—

Pay, *pave*, *pain*, *plain*, *paw*, *prawn*, *buy*, *bray*, *bane*, *brain*.

Gay, *gave*, *gain*, *glee*, *glean*, *Coe*, *cove*, *cone*, *clove*, *way*, *wave*, *wain*, *high*, *hive*, *day*, *dray*, *drain*, *drave*.

Tay, *tray*, *train*, *trance*, *transition*, *transitional*.

Other examples of the principle can be built up by the teacher or found in the various textbooks.

Imagination

This part of our subject cannot be dismissed without reference to the use and development of imagination as an educational factor. Children are often said to be imaginative, but they cannot imagine anything that has not been part of their experience. It may be argued that experience may be inherited; and, indeed, some of the natural impulses and reflex actions of man can be due to nothing but biological causes. In other words, education may begin before birth, and the teacher is at no time faced with a pupil whose mental outfit is free from impressions of some kind or other. No teacher can afford to ignore his pupil as an individual. We speak of the *average* pupil; but there is no such person. Class teaching is an attempt at striking an average; but the experienced teacher knows that, whilst some things are difficult for most pupils, there are some pupils who learn only by special treatment, generally an appeal to imagination. Success with the difficult is the test of the teacher.

Imagination and memory are closely allied; both are based on past experience. Memory reproduces past experience more or less faithfully; whilst imagination draws on experience and fits together a variety of ideas, raising up a new combination which may not be recognized as anything that has occurred before. Reproduction without recognition is imagination; reproduction with recognition is memory. Imagination is of value in shorthand in that the student may be trained to call up in imagination the outlines of new words based upon the similar words and symbols which he has already experienced. The mental picture of the familiar outline is due to memory, whilst that of the unfamiliar one is due to imagination.

Questioning

One of the most efficient adjuncts to any method of teaching is the *question*. It is, when properly used, a part of the reasoning, or, as it has been called, the development method. It is one of the best methods in use, and since the time of Socrates good questioning has never been discredited. The teacher should remember that the chief function of the question is to stimulate, to arouse curiosity and to awaken interest. To use it for discovering the extent of a student's knowledge is only a secondary function.

Questioning should be used to ascertain whether the class really understands the problem before it. It is useless to tell students that the final *s* sound in a word is represented by the circle o or the stroke) according to the principle of vowel indication, unless it is certain that each understands the expression "vowel indication." We are aware that a certain knowledge of the use of language is assumed; but here is a partially technical term which occurs in the textbook, and it is astonishing how glibly it is used and how few of the junior students really appreciate its meaning. If it is used at all, questions will settle whether the class understands its meaning. If the student has been taught to discover rules for himself, he will not use the expression; but he will understand it, if it is given as the teacher's interpretation of his students' *own* rule.

Where the textbook method is used, questioning is most valuable, since the teacher's duty is to expound and explain. A good method, questioning, does not necessarily improve a bad one—too much reliance on the textbook.

Strange words and badly constructed sentences cause confusion; let your language be simple and concise, clear and definite. Discourage guessing, although a good deal of inductive reasoning may amount to guesswork. Leading questions and elliptical questions are uneducational, and the legal question admitting of an answer "yes" or "no" is as unreliable as the toss of a coin. Every good question is thought-provoking and should be weighed carefully before being put.

In general, questions in class may be thought of in two categories. First there are those the teacher asks the class, or individuals in the class. These may be questions formed to stimulate curiosity and provoke thought so that correct mental relationships and associations may be formed. They may also be questions designed to find out how well the students have learned. Secondly there are the questions that the students ask the teacher. Broadly speaking the way of dealing with these is—

(*a*) If the question is a simple one asking for routine information or guidance, answer it simply and leave it at that.

(*b*) If the question is a thoughtful one raising important issues, encourage the questioner by commending him, give an answer and develop it by asking supplementary questions to involve the whole class in the matter raised.

(*c*) If the question betrays ignorance or a failure of understanding do not necessarily blame the questioner. Unless the question reveals gross inattention, the fault may well be your own, not the student's. Recapitulate. Build again the necessary process of step-by-step reasoning.

(*d*) If the question is one you cannot answer, then do not be afraid to say you do not know. Add, however, that you will find out the answer, and then be sure to do so

Individual and Group Teaching

Closely allied to the question of methods of teaching is the matter of individual and collective teaching. Each has its place in an educational scheme; but a judicious blending is by far the best.

The individual method takes cognizance of the individual as the unit, and this is right in all teaching; but in the hands of the inexpert, especially when numbers are to be considered, it very soon deteriorates into the correcting of exercises. Class teaching or group teaching has a stimulating effect, as it brings students together in quest of a common object. In this form of teaching the teacher can with wisdom take advantage of the natural impulses of rivalry, imitation, emulation and sociability, or herd instinct, all of which, as we have seen, can be elevating and useful in teaching.

Unfortunately, in our evening classes, dictates of economy provide our teachers with mixed classes, mixed as to knowledge, age and mental equipment. The only method suitable in cases of this kind is the individual method; but progress would be slow and teaching ineffective. In an hour's class, with thirty pupils, the limit would be two minutes each. To treat all as a class is unfair to the student who is in advance of his fellows, and to set the pace accordingly to the best equipped or the worst equipped is equally wrong. A rough division into three or four fairly homogeneous groups is the only practical solution, and the making of a programme to ensure an equal share of teaching and practice for each group is a logical sequel. Recourse to such a method, however, can lead only to a very limited success, and is fatiguing to the teacher, and lacking in stimulation to the student. It is not a good method for skill teaching.

Discipline

Discipline is very closely associated with method, and is really the bond which exists between readiness and method. Readiness to learn must be the primary attitude of the student, and discipline is a means of securing a constant state of readiness. Few teachers realize the true meaning of discipline. It is certainly not the physical condition of immobility, but rather the mental state of being willing to be taught. True discipline extends beyond the classroom doors, for willingness to be taught includes willingness to learn, and this naturally implies willingness to prepare work at home and to do exercises. The learning of short forms is not altogether a classroom task, and the disciplined student will help himself by practice on these outside school hours. It should be remembered that the whole of education is aimed at securing discipline or behaviour, that is, correct conduct in all emergencies of life. The teacher of commercial subjects has a hand in this important work. Try to inculcate discipline from within rather than from without. The correct physical attitude is of great importance; but it is unavailing unless accompanied by the correct mental attitude. (See Chapter III, page 19.) The natural impulses of the student must be restrained in order that teaching may prosper, and this is done by directing these impulses into proper channels. Keep the class occupied; expect the pupils to do much. Your province is to direct; theirs to do. Many teachers fail because they know their subject so well and have become so much a part of it that they take no account of the pupil. The rule should be pupil first, subject second, teacher last.

CHAPTER XI

CHOICE OF METHOD

THE choice of method of presentation is in the hands of the teacher and the teacher alone, since it is necessary to take into consideration the school and its nature, the class membership, times of meeting, weekly teaching periods and the whole class situation; present members' equipment, textbooks, notebooks, pens and pencils; as well as the teacher himself, his training, experience and exactness of knowledge. In spite of these diverse elements there are particular points common to all schools of the same type. For example, the broad facts of time allocation to shorthand work in evening classes vary little from institute to institute, a total of two or three hours weekly being the normal teaching time, and this with homework has to suffice. The class membership, however, varies and is affected by the daily labour of individual members, their age and educational background, so that it becomes necessary to have regard to the requirements of the individual as well as to the general classroom.

So long as this is kept in mind the method which in the judgment of the teacher is most effective for this purpose is the correct method to adopt. The teacher must, however, exercise his judgment and not merely take the line of least resistance. For the inexperienced, however, certain guiding lines can be laid down. Do not attempt to adhere strictly to any method to which a descriptive name can be applied. Forsake the traditional method or use it sparingly in spite of the diversity in the level of attainment and educational background of your class members. It is usually the line of least resistance and apparently the only visible way out, but it is usually wasteful, and the effectiveness of your teaching or supervising cannot well be tested through this method.

A combination of methods will be found most effective. Indeed the deductive method cannot be employed without the use of the inductive method. Vary your approach and presentation so as to keep interest alive. How can this be done with such a diversity of talent as usually goes to make up an evening class of beginners? A preliminary try-out will suffice for a rough classification into, say, three grades in which the policy of group teaching can be introduced. The secret of success in group teaching is to see that everyone is kept occupied. Each group should receive its class lesson and some of these may be general to the whole class. In a beginners' class it is always found good to deal generally with phonetic drill, penmanship, which includes correctness of slant, size and direction of outlines and strokes; and here the textbook is useful. From this point the graded sections each in turn have a short lesson and an assignment of work. Shorthand is learnt by doing, not talking, and the teacher's part may well be short. It will be found that as a session proceeds regrading is necessary both up and down, but let it appear in the latter case that the down grading is only for revision purposes.

There is a method of teaching shorthand in use in the United States of America which is definitely of value in the teaching situation disclosed in the beginners' stage in evening classes. This is the functional method. It is a pity that technical terms should need to be introduced into teaching practice, particularly such a term as "functional" which in educational work means "useful." However, this method is, in the hands of an expert teacher, as useful as any, but not more useful than the orthodox methods in use in our schools. Rules and principles are not taught and in the early stages reading practice only is given. No penmanship is allowed and the student learns by absorbing shorthand forms into the memory. The work is tested by transcription and no dictation is given at first. In other words the beginner is taught through reading correct shorthand forms. No doubt this method alone is slow and does not take into account the fact that in business life shorthand must be written *before* it is read. Yet a modification of this method is worth considering. The development of reading and writing abilities simultaneously is based on the educational principles we have already considered. The ultimate aim of most shorthand work is the correct transcript, which demands ability on the students' part to decipher their own notes. If the functional method be considered let the student from the first write his shorthand from printed plates with the simultaneous reading of the exercise by the teacher. This is a good exercise if carefully supervised and grading is immaterial. The student thus acquires a shorthand vocabulary through shorthand practice in accordance with the pedagogical laws of learning a skill subject. The steps are—

1. Read from the textbook, teacher first and then students together, in suitable small sections.

2. Re-read from textbooks, students in group and then individually.

3. Copy from textbook, a line of the textbook to a line of the notebook, leaving one or two lines blank after each copied line.

4. Copy again from the textbook to the teacher's dictation on alternate lines or on one line two or three times over.

5. Re-copy at a higher speed on the lines left blank.
6. Write from dictation without the copy.
7. Check and correct.

In the use of this method, rules may be a secondary consideration, being assimilated rather than taught formally. But the method can be used equally successfully with a preliminary instruction in the rules.

The following is the outline of two lessons based on the inductive principle to illustrate the teaching required in a lesson on the initial hooks to curves. A consideration of the outline given together with a description of the method set out in Chapter X should be valuable.

INITIAL HOOKS TO CURVES

This is Thursday. To-morrow will be ×

What word is ? Sound it. What sound is ?

Write: *fried, afraid, Fred, offer, freed, fraud.*

I.

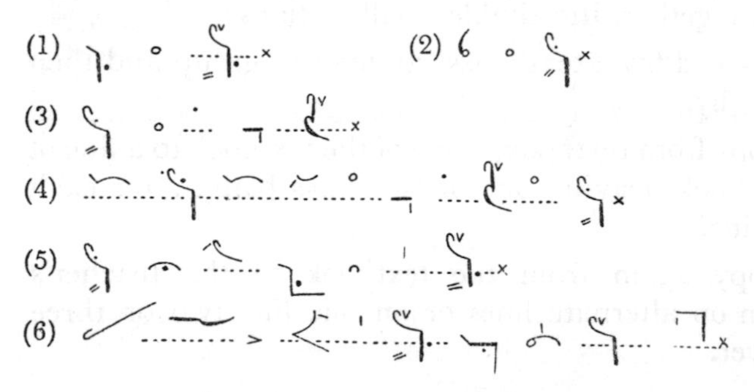

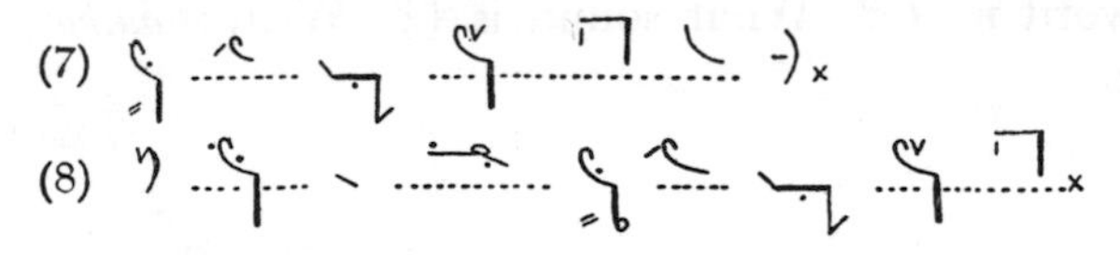

How is *r* added to a curve?

II. *Where are you going? I am going* [shorthand] *to my sister's house. She asked us to come* [shorthand] *to play bridge. She was* [shorthand] *here last and I agreed to go* [shorthand] *there to-night.*

What word is [shorthand]? What position is it in? Is it the usual position of a word with an *ō* vowel?

Look at the shorthand word in the next sentence and see if you can tell why *over* was not written in the usual position.

Have you [shorthand] *been to Radiolympia? Oh yes, I have gone there almost* [shorthand] *year since it started.*

What two words are represented by [shorthand]? Can you answer the question about *over* now?

(1)

(2)

(3)

(4)

(5)

(6) (7)

(8)

What word is [outline] ? What sound is [outline]? Write: *author, ether, either.*

III.

(1) 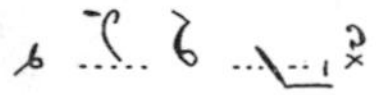 (2)

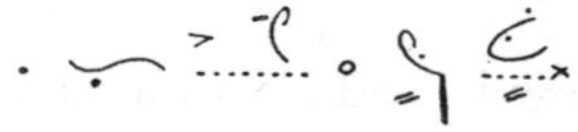

(3)

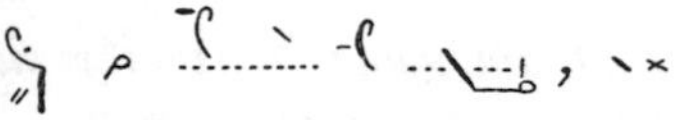

(4) 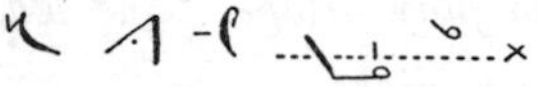 (5)

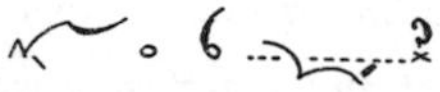

(6)

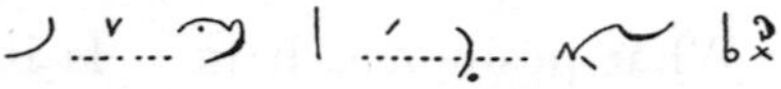

(7)

(8)

(9)

(10)

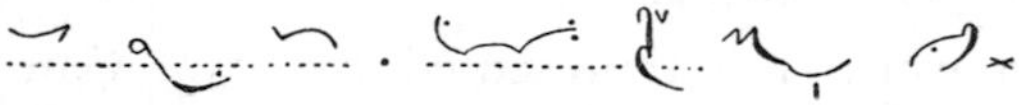

What sound is [outline]? Write: *treasure, pressure, usher.*

IV.

(1)

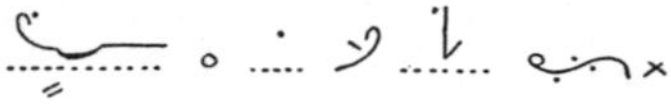

(2)

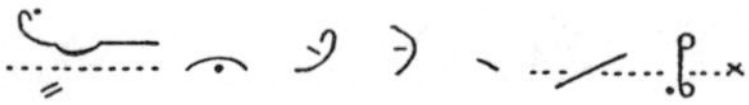

(3)  (4)

(5)

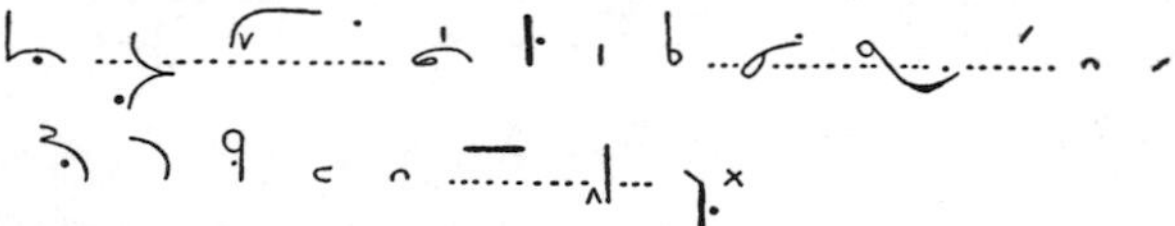

(6)

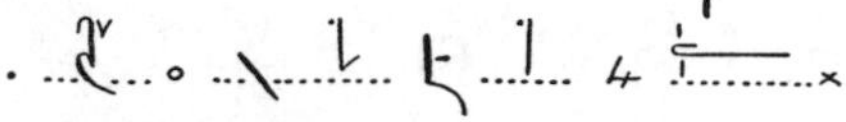

(7)

What word is ? What word is ? Write: *sinner, simmer, saner, signer.*

Ask if a decision has been reached. Is the decision a one, or may it be changed?

What sound is ?

Write: *panel, tunnel, journal.*

Read:

Review:

NEW LESSON. How many can you get right?

What is that you are reading? It is a story about the

Read: Copy.

Ask if he has his ticket for the theatre. says he has not. He says he to bring it. How could you your ticket ? You would your head if it were not fastened on. 'Phone home and tell John to bring ticket. Say to take it. I hope he won't to take the ticket.

What word is ? ? What does stand for?

Practice

Write: *Fred*
Fred forgot
Fred forgets

Two ways to write *fr*? Do you know the reason? Try to write + — in the air fast and + — in the air fast. Which is easier to read?

Watch out for other "duplicated" curves.

Read and copy—

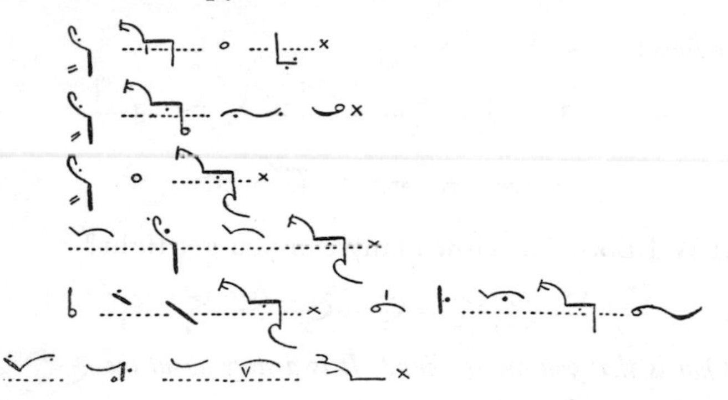

I promised to call Jim up and I to do so. Do you suppose he will ever me for forgetting? He will probably you if you have a good excuse. Did Jim you? Yes, he has me for I did have a really good excuse.

has a sister and a . The name is . and his are good friends. is older than . How much older is his ? His is two years older than .

Sometimes older *won't* *to play with younger* × *But* *is not like that.*

What word is it?

What does stand for? After which letter is written? Practise:

Where are you going? I am going into the garden to *flowers for the table. I always* *the flowers for the table. Here I have* *these. It rained while I was* *the flowers yesterday.*

What word is ? After what stroke is written in this word?

Practise: ×

Yesterday was Wednesday. To-day is × *is our maid's day out. On* *I am the cook. I am always glad when* *is over. I do not have time to* *flowers on* × *My* *them on* × *Where do you spend your* ? *We spend our* *at a place called Bethel.*

What word is ?

Read, copy, practise—

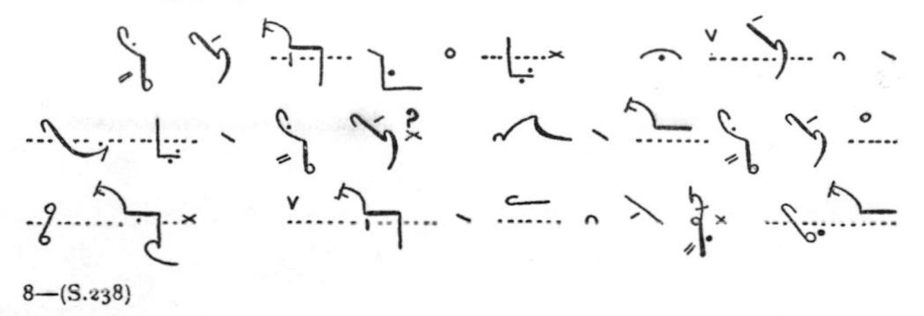

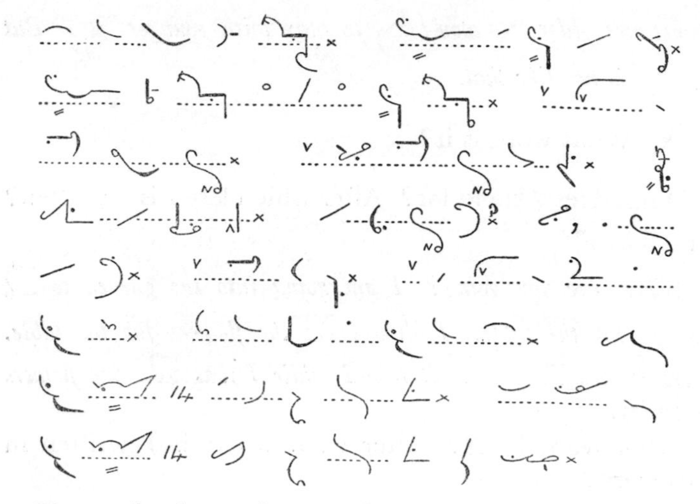

Please take the candy away ⌒\ *my desk. I can eat it* ⌒\ *morning till night. Once a week I receive a box* ⌒\ *Dad.*

What word is ⌒\? In what position is it?

Practise.

The new styles are ⌒\ *pretty. They are* ⌒\ *chic. The colours worn this season are* ⌒\ *gay. I like them* ⌒\ *much.*

What word is ⌒\? In what position is it?

What word is ⌒\? Do you know why ⌒\ is written this way and ⌒\ this way?

CHAPTER XII

SOME CONSIDERATIONS OF SPEED

THE most important mental attribute to a speed student is that of decision—indecision is fatal. The possession of sound theory and a knowledge of such possession must first be assured, and indecision will disappear.

Let us now consider the first rule of speed writing. Here I must warn the reader that not every speed-room teacher will agree with our rule, namely, *when a new word is heard in the course of dictation*, train your students to *write it at once, whether correctly or incorrectly*. Do it without hesitation; do not grope, but write and pass on. It may be urged against this advice that the student is thus laying the foundation for incorrect outlines; but it must be remembered that writing a word once does not set up a habit, and that the leaving of blanks in the shorthand note may become habitual. If only part of the outline be written, it is better than a blank, for the context may give the clue to the incorrect or incomplete outline. Remember, shorthand is a means and not an end. The point should be made that during the greater part of the actual training in writing at speed, the students should be writing only words that they know sufficiently well to be able to write them with technical correctness. Most speed practice should be prepared.

This suggestion is a dangerous one to follow unless it is pressed to its logical conclusion. Shorthand is written to be read or transcribed, and *no note should be taken that is not going to be read*. In reading, see that every student "rings" any incorrect or incomplete outline, always writing the correct form in the margin. Then let the corrected outline be the subject of repetition practice.

Repetition Without Interest

We have agreed that practice makes perfect, but the shorthand teacher should rather say: "*Good* practice makes perfect." What is good practice? Long acquaintance with shorthand and shorthand teachers and students has led the writer again and again to issue warning against *repetition without interest*, and in the early stages without thought. The following method is deprecated—

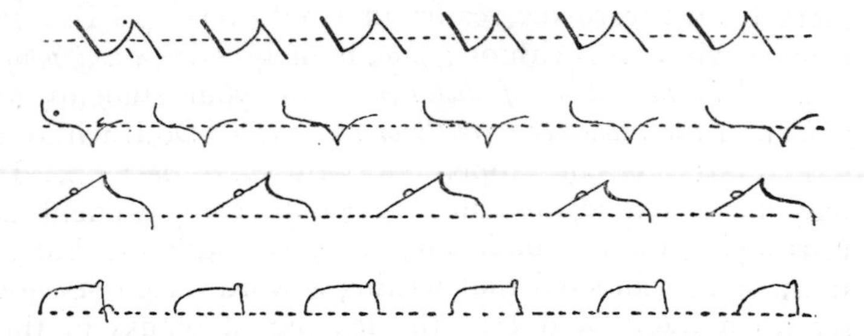

The reason for this attitude is the danger that an outline may deteriorate in the course of repetition, and finally, after from twelve to twenty repeats, may become indecipherable, while, at the same time, a habit may be set up which is bad and difficult to eradicate. Write the errors in shorthand fully vocalized in the margin of the notebook. Proceed downwards, writing the unvocalized outlines for the words one after the other and, coming back to the beginning, repeating as before—

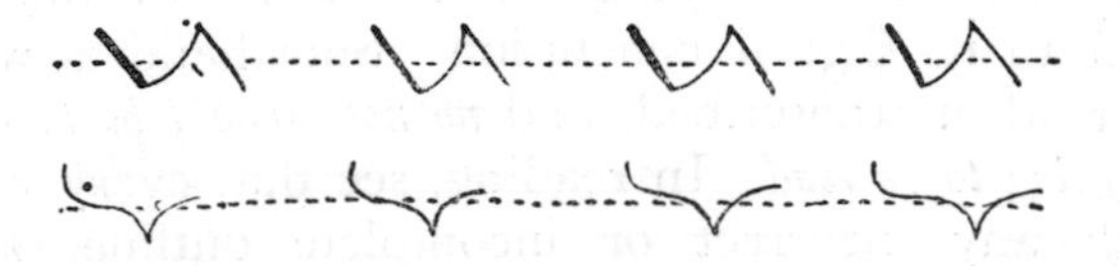

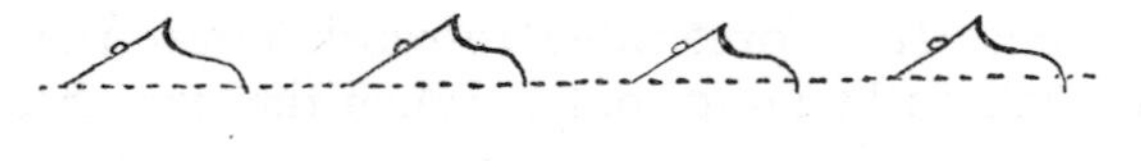

and so on.

Another way of ensuring that repetitive work should be performed with interest is to give the students a clearly defined goal to aim at and a precise time for its achievement.

Corrections and repetition work should be seen by the teacher, otherwise style of writing and facility in reading will suffer.

The teacher would do well to re-dictate the whole passage after repetition practice on corrected outlines, so that new words are again met in their context. Continuous writing should be the aim in every case.

Facility drill should form an important part of all speed preparation. For this purpose Facility Drills and Phrase Drill Books have been prepared by Sir Isaac Pitman & Sons Ltd., and the use of these prevents the deterioration of outline against which teachers are warned. The author of the *Phrase Drill Notebook* indicates in his preface the manner in which the book should be used and the method may be extended to all repetition work.

How to Use the Notebook

In each Drill in this book it will be found that there are five lines consisting of phrase signs, with three blank lines following each line of shorthand. The student should first read through the phrase signs given in a Drill, and then copy the signs carefully and neatly on the blank lines, repeating the words comprising the phrases as they are written. It is preferable to work *across* the page, writing each outline once only. When the page has been completed in this way, the student should repeat the process, writing the words and sentences many times. This subsequent writing can be done on top of the first. An effort should be made at each repetition to increase the speed of writing. The following illustration of the first linc of Drill One will demonstrate clearly the method suggested—

During this practice it should be kept in mind that a light touch is essential to successful shorthand writing. A heavy touch merely retards progress.

Regularity in Practice

For shorthand speed practice we have already suggested one hour each working day as the minimum. This is better than two hours on each of alternate days. It is realized that course syllabuses do not always allow such an arrangement, and, consequently, the teacher must act as guide, philosopher and friend. The two or three hours per week, which is the time probably allotted to him, must be devoted to strenuous work and to advice on outside practice. As adviser he should impress on his students that a little practice *each working day* is necessary.

William James, in his *Talks to Teachers*, says—

We forget that every good that is worth possessing must be paid for in strokes of daily effort. We postpone and postpone, until those smiling possibilities are dead. Whereas ten minutes a day of poetry, of spiritual reading or meditation, an hour or two a week of music, pictures or philosophy, provided we began *now* and suffered no remission, would infallibly give us in due time the fullness of all we desire. By neglecting the necessary concrete labour, by sparing ourselves the little daily tax, we are positively digging the graves of our higher possibilities. This is a point concerning which you teachers might well give a little timely information to your . . . pupils.

But William James would be the last person in the world to encourage preaching. Do not preach; but in your lesson refer to progress and the use to which its results can be put. Do not be afraid of reducing it to terms of £ s. d. Man is first and last a practical being.

Equally necessary is the weekly holiday, if the student is to maintain progress and avoid staleness.

Nowadays much may be done to ensure this regular daily practice by the use of sound-tapes, E.P. records, and the abundance of good material provided each week by *Pitman's Office Training*.

The student's work at home will depend entirely upon the availability of a reader. The acquisition of speed is difficult if he has to depend on lectures, sermons and speeches, for these are quite beyond his range in the initial stages; and, of course, it has long been recognized that the best form of training is steady, uniform, timed reading within the scope of his powers. Here the law of effect comes into play, and discouragement consequent on too high a rate of speed has a serious effect on the beginner, although occasionally to stretch him to the limits of his powers is a good exercise in good hands. After all, progress from one speed to a higher can come about only by the effort to do what we know when we set out is impossible for us. This is as true for the student struggling to reach 200 w.p.m. from 190 w.p.m. as it is for the student trying to "get" 60 w.p.m. having passed at 50 w.p.m.

The programme for a speed class period would be somewhat on the following plan—

1. Every Speed Class should be characterized by

(*a*) Sense of urgency and effort.

(*b*) Variety. No rigid pattern to the lesson.

(*c*) Sense of competitive effort and rivalry.

(*d*) Awareness of immediate and long term goals and objectives.

(*e*) Awareness of the individual and the problems of the individual.

(*f*) Hard work as much as from the student as from the teacher.

(*g*) Sense of achievement.

(*h*) Friendly and co-operative teacher/class relationship.

2. The Speed Class lesson should contain

(*a*) Some training in rapid reading from printed shorthand and from individual's shorthand notes or from the notes of other students. Reading techniques should be varied as much as possible.

(*b*) Short letter or memorandum (etc.) dictation to provide a vigorous start to the lesson. The matter may be taken from *Business Letters for Dictation* or from short (100 word) letters improvised, or from copies of actual correspondence.

(*c*) Drill on the short forms and phrases on a cyclic plan, i.e. a plan that ensures that no short forms are left for longer than a week or ten days unrevised. Use should be made of the lists provided in *Graded Dictation Studies*, and *The New Phonographic Phrasebook* and the *Grammalogue and Contraction Drill Notebook*.

(*d*) Specific penmanship and facility exercises (*Facility Notebook for Speed Students*). Attention should be given to particular defects e.g. roundness of strokes, especially of curved strokes, lightness of touch, etc.

(*e*) A brief four- or five-minute revision of some specific point of theory, e.g. *w*, *l* downward, all forms of *r*, treatment of *-ner*, etc. Use should be made of the *Student's Review*. This revision should be in a different form from the manner in which it was originally taught.

(*f*) Dictation. A considerable part of the dictation should be prepared, passages should be given in short one-minute bursts, repeated at increasing speeds, use should be made of the "Seen Passage" technique, of improvised dictation (increasing speed by ten words a minute every half-minute to a point twenty or thirty words a minute above the capacity of the class), of occasional longer sessions of continuous dictation (six or seven minutes well within the speed range of the class), of consolidation dictation repeating a passage already taken at a high speed at a lower speed, of dictation from tape recordings, and dictation by different voices. Part of the training should also include practice in retention. Sentences of gradually increasing length should be dictated and the students required to record them *after* the dictation has finished.

(*g*) Occasional copied-dictation from *Pitman's Office Training*. This still has value in increasing the student's vocabulary.

(*h*) Occasional transcription exercises in class. These should be brief and may be checked sometimes in class and sometimes by the teacher. When transcription is checked by the teacher it is most important that it should be thoroughly checked and properly corrected.

Correction has no point if the students do not learn from the correction.

3. During Speed Classes teachers should be sure to provide their students with specific information about the nature of the various examinations available to all students who should be encouraged to regard the test of an examination as the only qualification worth having. The length of the test and the types of matter should be clearly indicated and illustrated in practice.

4. Teachers should, either alone or in co-operation with other teachers, build up a stock of dictation material of as varied a character as possible.

5. All students in Speed Classes should purchase *Pitman's Office Training* weekly. The shorthand material should be used throughout for reading practice, for dictation preparation, and for theory revision. With more advanced students the shorthand is also very useful for fair-copying work.

6. The following are suggestions for dictation material:

Letters: *Business Letters for Dictation; Dictation Practice in Business Correspondence.*

Literary: 700 *Common-Words Dictation Book*; *Second Session Dictation Course*; Suitably amended extracts from *Reader's Digest*, *The Sunday Times*, *The Observer*, *The Listener*, etc. (Care needs to be taken to standardize the difficulty of vocabulary and syntax.)

Company Reports: *Elementary Examination Speed Tests* (rather difficult matter at low speeds including plenty of figures). 700 *Common-Words Dictation Book* (very good as an introduction to Company Reports). *The Financial Times* often has articles and reports which contain much of the usual vocabulary of this type of material.

Parliamentary: *Second Session Dictation Course*; old copies of *Hansard* (H.M.S.O.).

Economic: *The Financial Times*, *The Economist*, *The Sunday Times*, *The Observer*, Bank Reviews. (These are usually obtainable monthly and gratis from the Banks.)

7. Shorthand must be written in a proper shorthand notebook.

8. Teachers should seek to secure a proper balance between the various activities of the Speed Class. Generally speaking not more than half the total time should be devoted to dictation. Apart from the periods of consolidation during which students are writing from the spoken word at a rate well within their capacity, the dictation periods should be regarded as the peaks of effort during the class.

Theory Revision

The usual plan in the speed room is to deal with difficult outlines as they arise in the course of dictation, and the theory revision proposed will not interfere with this practice. What is here suggested is a systematic revision taking the student through the theory, lesson by lesson, and dictating *at speed* an exercise based on the revision. The revision may be by way of question and answer, and the exercises selected may be taken from a textbook other than that used in the theory class; or, better still, they may be the teacher's own exercises, selected to suit his plan of revision. If he prefers a textbook, and the *New* or *Modern Course* is the class textbook, let him work through the *Commercial Course* or the *Student's*

Review. This theory revision should not be desultory, but should be regular and systematic, to the end that in the speed class the student will work through the exercises selected at least twice in the course. He thus reviews the course, and this covers the whole of the subject matter and the principles of the system, and increases vocabulary, whilst the dictation prepares him for taking continuous matter later in the lesson.

Speed Dictation

Variety is fundamental to this important part of the class lesson. Here the personality and taste of the teacher should have free play, subject to certain conditions, namely—

1. Subject-matter should be carefully selected and varied in character, so that the student's vocabulary may be gradually built up. The majority of our students are either in business or destined for business life, so that business letters and commercial matter, such as company-meeting reports, market reports, and the like, will possibly predominate. Political matter, leading articles and literary matter must not, however, be neglected.

2. The matter should be carefully counted in quarter-minutes for various speeds, the most convenient marking being that which is shown in the following passage, counted at 80 words per minute—

> *As you know, gentlemen, this is the statutory meeting which we are obliged to hold under the Companies Act; there | is no resolution to put before you, and there is really no business to be transacted. We put this statement | before you, and we show that all the regulations according to the Companies Act have been carried out up to | the present time. It is, however, very gratifying to see so many shareholders here, and I would like to take | the opportunity of telling you as much as we know of the estate at the*

present time. We received a | telegram on 5th January reporting that the estate had been taken over from the previous owners, so that we have | no estate information to give you at present, but the preliminary report which has been sent shows that the estate | is in thoroughly good order, and bears out in every respect the statement which was issued in lieu of prospectus. |

Other methods of marking the material for dictation are also useful:

(i) Marking in tens. An experienced teacher may then use the material at any required speed.

(ii) Marking the material (for test passages) in conventional paragraphs of quarter- or half-minutes in typescript separated by two line spaces.

(iii) Leaving the material unmarked but clipping a separate margin on the sheet indicating at the end of every second or third line how many seconds should have elapsed on arrival at that point.

3. Do not guess the speed. Even the most expert reader cannot read accurately to time without reference to a watch or speed clock.

4. Do not neglect the short commercial letter, transcription of which is, after all, the end of most of our shorthand teaching.

Speed Tests

The utilization of the time available for speed practice is in the hands of the teacher; but he should *occasionally* use it in such a manner that what he does may be emulated by his students in their homework. The repetition plan described below is not intended to occupy every hour of speed practice; but much would be gained if, once a fortnight, work on the lines suggested were taken up and followed by students at home with their own reader. Speed matter should be counted in one-, three-, five-, and seven-minute pieces. The one-minute pieces are for repetition practice; the three- and five-minute pieces for occasional dictation; and the seven-minute pieces for examination preparation, and for the testing of staying powers. These will be read, the student will take notes, and the notes should be alternately read back and transcribed. Short pieces should predominate. The transcription under the circumstances of evening-class work will be a home exercise with very occasional class transcripts. Each piece should be checked. Errors, whether mishearing, motor inco-ordination, English, punctuation or missing outline, should be corrected, and the corrections should be practised assiduously. *No speed matter should ever be read which is not intended for reading back or transcribing.*

The teacher is recommended to use the *Shorthand Teachers' Supplement* issued for the benefit of teachers of Pitman's shorthand and providing each month sufficient dictation material for all general purposes.

Repetition Work

The special routine repetition work mentioned above will be done on one-minute pieces or facility exercises. One-minute pieces should be dictated at the highest speed of the room. Students will find it hard at first; but they should be encouraged to write as if their future job depended upon getting down the whole article. Teach them to aim at putting down something. On the higher speed readings, style, phrasing, size of notes and all the other niceties which are usually and ultimately of supreme importance should be banished to the background, rather than the student should fail to get down something for everything that he hears.

Reading Back

The next step is the reading back of the note, which should be done quickly, each individual in the class taking his share. The teacher should be ready to ask the question: "What outline have you for that word?" "Did you phrase that?" "Did you use the right contraction there?" "What is the rule in such cases?" Let students note each mistake made, writing correctly in the margin all words which they have written incorrectly. Pay some attention to elementary phrasing; but do not be tempted to overdo this if the word habit seems to have become definitely fixed. Give a few minutes' repetition practice on the outlines that have been rewritten, *and see the students' notebooks*. Give a word of praise here, and, if necessary, of admonition there; and, finally, prepare to read the piece again. Read the test a second time, keeping well within the speed of the lowest in the room. This time attention should be given to correct phrasing, to style, that is, perfection in form and size of outlines; and, finally, to the incorporation of the corrected outlines in the new note. The reading back on this occasion should take a much shorter time. Corrections should be few; but reading and corrections should not be neglected, although the matter will be read again. The third reading should be again pushed to the maximum; but the result on this occasion should be very different from that which was shown on first reading. There should be no taking down "just anything," no incomplete or inaccurate outlines, and no careless errors. If time permits, the same piece may well be taken again; but, if not, it is a good plan to make it a first reading at the next lesson, this time slightly above any previous speed. The writer has seen a class nominally writing 70 words per minute take a piece on the foregoing plan, letting a day elapse between each reading, and at the end of four days it was taken at 90 words per minute by the whole class with less than 2 per cent of error.

The foregoing is not an hourly programme; but it is a programme which might well be followed occasionally in class and by the student working with his own reader, for the pupil who has sufficient interest to solicit the help of another has an interest strong enough to succeed on lines such as have been suggested, which would, but for motive, and knowledge of the specific goal to be aimed at approach something near to drudgery.

Learning Short Forms

Another branch of the routine work in the speed room should be regular exercises on short forms.

In classes where the *Modern Course* or the *New Course in Pitman's Shorthand* has been used in the theory stage the acquisition of the short forms and other arbitrary signs should give no trouble. The exercises have been continuous matter and constant practice of the arbitrary signs has in consequence been given so that the ancient bugbear of learning short forms out of context is unnecessary. Nevertheless, it is good and salutary practice to test the short forms regularly in isolation from context at regular speeds of 60 words a minute and upwards.

The following exercise contains all the single-stroke short forms the student should have at his pen point.

One paragraph is sufficient dictation of this kind of matter at a class meeting—

My Dear Doctor,

During our talk this morning you asked me to give you in writing my opinion of your scheme, and it is a very great pleasure to me to do so. I am sure it is an important improvement, and that it will be a very good thing for myself and equally so for every gentleman who may wish to improve himself in those things which stamp a man as a gentleman among gentlemen. I do not see how there can be much difference of opinion on the subject. It appears to me impossible to suggest improvements except of a general character. However, I shall take advantage of any particular opportunity which may present itself, during the next month or two, of putting the principle to the test, as a mere generalization does not always represent the truth.

I think I ought to tell you that, with the exception of Mr. Smith, I believe all our members share my opinion. When asked what would be the effect of turning down the suggestion, he remarked, with rather more spirit than usual, that he did not care to say.

I have just remembered that I have an appointment to visit a number of our northern branches, and within the next fortnight I must make a valuation of a large building used in connexion with the first and largest of our southern branches. Owing to the fact that trade has been very brisk during most of the year, we are compelled to build still larger premises.

It may surprise you to be told that over two-thirds of our establishments report wonderful increases in business when compared with last year. This is a cause for great cheer, and is due largely to the influence of several new advertisements which we have tried during the winter.

I will take the liberty of showing you the figures when next you call. I am sure you will agree that they speak for themselves. They are very instructive, and have given us great satisfaction. I myself took care to send instructions to the copy-writer to put in hand at once a further series, the first of which will appear on Monday next.

Under the circumstances, I felt I must thank him on my own behalf, as well as on behalf of my partners, who are abroad, and who cannot therefore speak for themselves, for the wonderfully fine and difficult work he has done for us. He is quite young, and he tells me that when at school he gave special attention to the study of modern languages and commercial subjects. This is significant, and beyond doubt has proved of great advantage to him: exactly how much it is impossible to say. By the way, I think he would be surprised to see that I had inscribed myself as "Yours very sincerely."

A new design for a poster has been delivered here. It shows a child walking towards a chair, but, though satisfactory as far as mere technique is concerned, it has neither the significance nor the appeal which will attract the people whose good word we desire, and it must, therefore, be improved.

The idea is altogether too subjective, and there is no justification for including unusual words. We must guard against being old-fashioned, although schooled in the use of what is correct in an inscription. Thus, "Oh, may I have a gold watch eh, mother?" would, although not awe-inspiring, appeal to the selfish instinct which is inherent in everyone, no matter how much they may disclaim selfishness. There is no reason why the new poster should be more than a yard square, as even then it would not be equalled by any others near at hand. It can be made to accord with the sentiment expressed by Dr. Rose, which was cheered at our last annual meeting. I expect you remember the enthusiasm created. The Doctor might almost have been chaired had the occasion been a festive one and high spirits not held in subjection.

Lord Howe called an hour ago. He said he could not come according to appointment because he was suffering from a cold. He wished to know whether, if he placed a number of export orders in the near future, we should be able to deliver them towards the end of the year. I signified that we ourselves, as principals, might be willing, but we should be principally influenced by the information supplied by our agents, and must wait till we had their report. On terminating his call his lordship remarked: "Ah, well, I owe you nothing now."

Normal Routine

In the normal speed practice which should form the general routine of the class, whilst no dictation should be given which is not to be read back or transcribed, it is equally important that no matter should be taken down in shorthand that is not to be corrected. The corrections should be handled in the way already described; a ring should be placed round the wrong outline, and the corrected form should be written in the margin. This should then be drilled, using the plan already described on page 108. If it were not for the interest which is to be aroused, this practice would be nothing but drudgery; but the alert teacher will see to it that it is not in any way looked upon as anything but pleasant and progressive exercise.

Passages selected for dictation may be used again, provided they are not used too frequently, and provided the matter does not get out of date. There is no interest for the student in taking down passages about the political position during the War. Let your students' speed matter be up to date, whether it be business, political, economic or general. The only kind of matter that is not dated is literary. As already stated, this kind should not be forgotten. Finally, although examiners set passages of four, five and seven minutes' duration, much teaching can be done effectively with less lengthy ones.

Preparation of Speed Matter

It has already been suggested that errors should be detected before they are made. A competent teacher knows at once the unfamiliar word that may cause hesitation. It is his business to come to class prepared. A piece of speed matter should not be read without the teacher being thoroughly familiar with all its difficulties. He should collect the difficulties beforehand and deal with them before the piece is read. But this is not sufficient. They must be again collected from the transcripts and notes, and made the subject of a *short* talk and further drill.

In the speed room, as in the theory room, much can be done by utilizing the instincts of rivalry, pride, imitation and emulation. Even with senior students, the giving of a place and grading arouses interest. The plan, therefore, to be adopted by the teacher is to prepare his speed matter beforehand; to go to his room ready to consider possible difficulties; to dictate, to correct, drill on errors, re-dictate; and, finally, to grade his class according to results. No transcript is worth having unless it shows below 2 per cent of error. The spirit of emulation is fostered by asking for correct transcripts and by displaying satisfactory notes on the notice-board. The notice-board in the class-room, if carefully used, is one of the most satisfactory means of encouragement.

Fair Copy

Some time during *every speed period*, and, most particularly, during the period in which repetition practice has been taken should be devoted to fair copying. The reading and writing of shorthand from well-executed printed shorthand material is a very important part of the speed-student's training. The mental image of well-written shorthand outlines is in itself a stimulus to good form. The object of the fair-copy writer is to make a duplicate copy of the shorthand taken either from the textbook or from *Pitman's Office Training*. The object of this work is to check any tendency to deteriorate in style, and if writing fair copy becomes a habit there will be no difficulty in making it a part of the actual speed practice. The fair copying required should be specific in length and the time allowed for it definite. If class instruction is then focused on two or three lines only of the fair copy, individual students may be given helpful criticism and their attention directed to weaknesses of penmanship.

Students should be encouraged to read as much printed

shorthand as possible, as shorthand reading is next in importance to shorthand writing. It is a good plan in a speed class to excite interest and promote a healthy rivalry. For instance, on occasions a short passage may be read, and students may be allowed to change notes and to transcribe each other's work, keeping in view the one important point, that for business purposes the end of a shorthand note is a typescript or a longhand transcript.

Speech and Vocabulary

The subject-matter of shorthand teaching is the spoken word, and progress in acquiring shorthand depends somewhat on vocabulary. Although one of the difficulties in the early stages is to make students realize that the written word has little to do with Pitman's shorthand, the shorthand teacher in the long run has the advantage over the primary teacher who is endeavouring to teach spelling to young children. Pitman's shorthand is rational in its aims, whilst the English language as written and printed has a spelling far from rational. The ability to spell is not necessary in making a shorthand note; but, as shorthand is a means to an end, and that end is the ultimate provision of a transcript, say, a typewritten letter, in ordinary popular characters, the ability to spell is closely related to the rendering of a perfect transcript. The shorthand teacher must not divorce his subject from English and spelling, and he should use every opportunity of giving assistance in both these subjects. Poor shorthand is blamed for many of the errors found in the work of the shorthand-typist and of the speed class; but the bulk of such errors will occur if the writer takes his notes in longhand from slow dictation.

Growth of Vocabulary

Vocabulary, which is an important matter in shorthand teaching, is acquired in four stages. First through the ear, then through speech, later through the eye, and, finally, through movement of the muscles. The ear vocabulary commences before the child can talk, and it continues to grow throughout life. The oral vocabulary commences with the first spoken word, and it is drawn naturally from the aural (ear) vocabulary. The teaching of reading introduces the pupil to the third stage in the acquirement of a word list. With the average person the vocabulary acquired through the eye is not so extensive as the aural and oral vocabularies; but in the person of wider experience and deep reading this may well provide the most extensive of his vocabularies. Finally, the written vocabulary becomes a part of the pupil's mental make-up. This is the shortest of all. A student may know words through the eye and through the ear; but neither in speech nor in writing are they used. It is a function of the teacher of shorthand to increase the written vocabulary and to bring it as nearly to the aural one as possible. It has been said that *one* of the secrets of high-speed writing is a good general education, and this is true in so far as a command of words is part of a good general education.

We must assume in our teaching of theory that our students are ordinary persons with an ordinary vocabulary, and on this assumption let our exercises be chosen from such a vocabulary. Do not use words which are unfamiliar and unusual merely for the sake of illustrating an exception to a rule which has otherwise an almost universal application. Let such an exception take care of itself until such time as the principles as a whole are mastered, and by such time the student will be in a position to provide for the exception. (See Chapter XI.)

Aims of Shorthand Teaching

The aims of shorthand teaching are two of those common to teachers of longhand writing, namely, legibility and speed. The third aim in the ordinary school handwriting should be individuality; but in shorthand writing this can be ignored as an aim, as it will assert itself in due course.

The demand, for a universal style seems to be almost an impossible one. Nevertheless, the best and most easily transcribed note is the one which conforms most nearly to the geometrical style of the textbook and the lithographed page. The only definite rule that can or should be laid down is that scribbled and unwieldy outlines are not conductive either to easy reading or easy writing. We have already suggested in the section on "Habit Formation" that under certain circumstances the student should "get something down." But this does not mean write *anyhow*. It merely means that the student should form the habit of taking down rather than of leaving blanks. It may be suggested that "getting something down" of everything that is heard will lead to guessing; but it should be remembered that the expert reader of longhand does not actually see every word he reads, and half his reading is guesswork. In fact, in the higher realms of study one-half of so-called inductive reasoning is guessing.

Styles of Writing

What is the best style to adopt in speed writing? The answer partly depends upon the individual. Sometimes throughout a whole school a neat, small style of note will be found, whilst in another school a bold and flowing style will be paramount. Either is satisfactory provided that the former does not become cramped, so checking the free movement of the hand so necessary in speed writing, and that the latter does not become sprawly, with too few outlines to the line, entailing jumping from line to line and the constant turning of pages. The most successful writers at high speed almost invariably have a small neat style in which light cursive free writing is combined with a continuous control, no matter how great the pressure.

The subject is admirably discussed in the preface to *High-speed Shorthand Round The World*, the whole of which is indispensable for the shorthand teacher.

Notebooks for Speed

A word may be said as to notebooks. Most speed writers favour a narrow book, and this has its advantages. It entails frequent changing of lines but set against this is the preservation of continuity and the fact that the forearm has not to be shifted. The writer does not go back so far with a narrow book and the balance is in its favour. The widest book that is convenient is one of 5½ in., and this should have a 1 in. margin for corrections. The paper should always be of high quality so that it is virtually impossible for a pen to scratch or catch in the surface. Notebooks should not be thick as writing deteriorates if the hand has to be lifted far above the resting point of the arm.

Reading

Teachers tend to emphasize writing shorthand at the expense of reading it, yet every practising high speed writer will assure you that reading correct shorthand is of paramount importance in building vocabulary, consolidating theoretical knowledge and assisting in raising the rate of writing. Reading should begin (for the less experienced writer) with careful concentration on all outlines that cause hesitation, but it should always be repeated until the speed of reading is as rapid as the words may be enunciated. Fast writers often read the passage five or six times, timing themselves by the stopwatch first for oral reading and later for eye-reading. Ample reading practice is regularly available in *Pitman's Office Training*. Many literary works are also available in shorthand.

CHAPTER XIII

TEXTBOOKS

It is often suggested that the textbook provided for a given subject determines the method of teaching that subject, but this should not be the case. It may to a certain extent determine the order in which the material is presented, but it cannot in the long run determine method, unless the teacher adheres to what has been called the traditional textbook method of teaching, that is, the learning of rules as presented in the books, the consideration of examples following the rules and the working of exercises from the book. This method standing alone is rightly discredited. The proper function of the textbook is to provide the material upon which to work.

As in every other subject there is a choice of textbooks. These textbooks, each containing the principles of the system developed to a greater or lesser degree of completeness, have been compiled for various different purposes.

The *Modern Course in Pitman's Shorthand* with its companion *Drill Notebooks* offers a course of training on a 700 word vocabulary and bases its usefulness on the idea that common words constantly repeated in context form the backbone of a sound knowledge and ability to use Pitman's shorthand.

The *Instructor*, on the other hand, is a complete exposition of all the principles of Pitman's shorthand and is a textbook formed by the combination of what are known as the *Shorthand Manual* and the *Reporter*. It is offered to the teacher as his *vade mecum* of shorthand, and to the student who desires by self-tuition to make himself master of the subject for reporting and similar work.

The *Modern Course* by itself may be hardly sufficient for the commercial student who desires to become an effective shorthand writer, whilst it is not necessary to have the fullness of the latter book for this purpose. The learner from the *Modern Course* will increase his shorthand vocabulary after firmly fixing the general rules by continuing his studies through *A Student's Review of Pitman's Shorthand*. There is also an intermediate book known as the *Commercial Course* in use, presenting the system as a whole but not detailing in minute particulars some of the rules, leaving this detail if it is at all essential to be supplied by the teacher. This handbook is recommended for use by older students in day schools where the conditions of the time-table are such that plenty of time can be given to shorthand as a vocational subject, say, five, seven, to a maximum of ten class periods per week.

Whilst it is perfectly true that the order of presentation should not affect teaching methods, and, whilst the textbook merely contains the matter and not the method of teaching, an attempt has recently been made to present the subject-matter in a more modern dress, eliminating the writing of longhand and the working of long exercises, basing the examples on a vocabulary of the 2,000 commonest words used, but providing occasional additional illustrations from less frequently occurring words. The principles are offered in a logical form and they are stated briefly and simply with an adequate amount of application. This presentation is known as the *New Course*, and is a deservedly popular textbook for student and teacher alike. The *New Course* has valuable supplementary books such as *Facility Drills* (in two parts), the chief purpose of which is to develop penmanship speed and skill through the link of simultaneous seeing and hearing. There is also a most useful volume, particularly for teachers, called

Graded Dictation Studies, an almost indispensable companion to the *New Course*, compiled on exactly parallel lines chapter by chapter with the *New Course*. It contains a large amount of dictation material graded by word frequency and having the words numbered in tens for dictation at any speed. Dictation material is also provided for the short forms and phrases.

The principle of continuing the theory of shorthand throughout the course by means of short revision lessons at what is generally known as the speed stage can well be followed by the teacher using as his own handbook either the *Instructor* or *A Student's Review of Pitman's Shorthand*. This last-named provides additional vocabulary, and has an introduction which is useful to the teacher, as it places before the reader the main problems which are met in the shorthand classroom. The order of presentation is somewhat different from that used in the other textbooks, but here the order in which the principles are given does not matter, as the student is supposed to have the groundwork of every principle prior to undertaking work as presented in *A Student's Review of Pitman's Shorthand*. Thus the forms popularly known as "initial hooks," representing the commonest combinations of letters in the English language, are dealt with at the beginning of the book. These are followed by other hooked forms so that the whole of this principle of attaching a hook to a stroke is laid before the student as one section. There is the further advantage that all the points concerned with a single shorthand representation, e.g. whether to write the consonant upwards or downwards, are brought together for analysis and comparison.

A further work of the highest value as a general revision of the system is *The New Phonographic Phrasebook*. As its title implies, this volume deals systematically with the whole theory and practice of phrasing, but in fact it proves in use to go much farther than this, and is a "follow-up" like *A Student's Review* from which the more advanced student will derive great benefit.

The choice of the right textbook depends upon a number of factors such as the age and general educational background of the students, the time available for study, the final purpose of the course, the competence and methods of the teacher, and so forth. Any shorthand teacher or prospective teacher can readily obtain guidance and confirmation on this important subject by writing to the Service Manager, Sir Isaac Pitman & Sons Limited, 39 Parker Street, London, W.C.2.

CHAPTER XIV

ARE ANY OF THESE QUESTIONS YOURS?

THE questions that follow are of the kind often asked at conferences and courses for teachers of commercial subjects. Brief answers are suggested with some references to other parts of the text.

QUESTION 1

Why are there so many shorthand textbooks and which do you advise for—

(*a*) A secondary school with five teaching periods per week.

(*b*) An independent school with eight teaching periods.

(*c*) Evening classes with two teaching periods of 1–1½ hours each?

ANSWER 1

Refer to Chapter XIII.

(*a*) The *Modern Course* with its associated *Drill Notebooks*, or the *New Course* used in conjunction with the *New Course Intensive Workbook* and *Graded Dictation Studies* (for the teacher) would be suitable.

(*b*) The *Commercial Course* which can be used with *Reading Exercises on the Commercial Course*, and with *Graded Speed Tests for Shorthand Students* (Charlesworth), or the *New Course* with its associated books as in (*a*) above.

(*c*) The *New Course* with its subsidiary books would be sufficient. It is important to encourage students to read and write at least one exercise a day under the conditions quoted.

The reason for the variety of shorthand textbooks is, of course, the need to satisfy various purposes and to provide for the different ages and abilities of students.

QUESTION 2

How should I plan my lessons for an evening class of so-called beginners, having a variety of types of student when measured in terms of shorthand knowledge and general education?

ANSWER 2

It is best to try to keep the class together as a unit for as long a time as possible. When the gaps in knowledge and skill open out in spite of all that can be done, the class will have to be graded into two or three groups of roughly homogeneous students. Group teaching with individual attention to students will now have to be adopted. If other groups of beginners are studying at the same time, a system of regrading and promotion should be introduced.

QUESTION 3

How should I test my pupils?

ANSWER 3

Tests can be of two kinds, formal and informal. There is a danger, however, of speaking of the general work in class as being in the nature of a test. This should be avoided. Most shorthand teachers test their students too often. The formal tests should take place at well-spaced points. The frequency of the informal tests set by the teacher for his own benefit and for the purpose of grading will depend upon the number of teaching periods per week. Some teachers prefer to test after completion of a principle. Some prefer to test on the basis of time. Much depends upon the purpose for which tests are conducted.

The procedure whether the test is formal or informal should be careful preparation by the teacher beforehand, not the selection fortuitously of any piece of reading matter. The tests should be fair, and should not consist of exceptions and traps. They should cover the whole of the ground dealt with to the time of the test and should not incorporate words outside the vocabulary of the average students in the class. Most tests in these days will be from dictation. Even in theory tests the major portion should consist of dictated matter. See also the answer to Question 8.

QUESTION 4

How should I mark tests?

ANSWER 4

The marking of a test which records only deductions for error without indicating the nature of the error is unsatisfactory. In the course of marking, the type of error should where possible be indicated, and a definite scheme should be drawn up. If 100 marks be given for the whole of a paper complete errors can be penalized by marks being deducted to a number depending upon the nature of the error. Thus, an error in vowel or position might mean the deduction of one mark, an error of transcription one mark, a grammalogue or short-form error three marks, word wholly wrong three marks; omission of a group of words might be penalized by, say, one mark for each three words omitted, marking here depending entirely on whether the reason for the omission can be grasped from the transcript itself. An error in consonant, that is, a stroke or alternative form, or substitution of one consonant for another, two marks. This could be drawn up into a table which the teacher could do himself. Thus—

3 consonants wrong, multiply by 2, equals . . .	6
4 vowels or position wrong, multiply by 1, equals .	4
3 grammalogues wrong, multiply by 3, equals . .	9
Omission of 5 words, divided by 3, equals . .	2
Total deduction	21
Deduction from 100	79
Appropriate mark for paper therefore	79

Seventy or seventy-five marks remaining would be a reasonable pass. Some teachers adopt a different scale. In marking theory papers one teacher allows 20 complete errors before judging a theory paper to be a failure, and marks on the following basis—

Direct infringement of a rule	1 error
Wrong position of outline or incorrect vowel .	½ error

Repetition of the same error is not to be penalized.

Another teacher penalizes to the extent of ½ for a wrong vowel, vowel in the wrong position or an outline in the wrong position, an incorrect outline being penalized a full mark. If a reasonable outline is written, not breaking a rule already learnt, although not in conformity with the accepted method of writing, no penalty is exacted.

In the marking of a speed test the question of penalizing for spelling and punctuation must be taken into consideration. In general the shorthand note is not considered, the transcript being the main test. In the course of informal tests or class tests this policy is wrong, but for examinations and grading no doubt the transcript should be the most important matter. The views on penalties are as diverse as the number of possible types of error in a speed test, and the following is a rough table upon which marking can be based—

Transcription must agree word for word with original dictation unless an accidental deviation from copy is made in the dictation and explained in a statement submitted with the papers.

Any deviation in punctuation, paragraphing or capitalization will be allowed if it conforms to established usage.

One penalty for each of the following errors—

1. Omitted word.
2. Added word.
3. Substituted word.
4. Transposition of words if sense of sentence is altered, or standards of good English are infringed.
5. Use of longhand in shorthand note.
6. Erasure of longhand in note and replacement by shorthand.
7. Error in capitalization.
8. Error in punctuation.
9. Mis-spelled word.
10. Unauthorized abbreviations.
11. Figure misplaced.
12. Figure omitted.

All sums are counted as words, e.g. £67,347,248 omitted would be fifteen errors.

Wherever possible, something more than an indication of marks deducted for error is required. There is a tendency for students to work on the idea that errors do not matter so long as they do not count up to the margin of failure. The aim in shorthand is perfect accuracy and all marking should be directed to making the pupil error-conscious by directing attention to mistakes rather than marks.

Correction or marking of any kind does not complete the teacher's problem. Corrected work must be studied, remedies suggested for errors, and general mistakes become the basis of a short lesson and drill.

QUESTION 5

What would you give as homework exercises?

ANSWER 5

Where possible the teacher should avoid giving new shorthand outlines as part of a homework exercise. All new shorthand should be as far as possible done under supervision so that faulty outlines and errors of principle may immediately be eliminated. Unless done under supervision, shorthand errors tend to be repeated and are very difficult to correct. The following types of exercise may most usefully be set for work at home—

(i) Fair copying of previously read exercises.

(ii) Written drills on short forms and the essential phrases to bring them to the condition of "overlearning."

(iii) Occasional short transcriptions (transcriptions done at home or out of class should never be accepted as "passing" tests at given speeds of shorthand dictation) Transcription of printed shorthand (*Pitman's Office Training*) is good practice in small doses.

(iv) Reading practice and preparation. The adequacy of the work done will depend very much on the standard required in class when the work is checked.

(v) Preparation for dictation. This work is useful at every stage but particularly after the theory when speed is being developed. The preparation can take various forms; the copying and re-copying of certain lines or sections where facility of execution is more difficult, the repetition of the less common words and phrases to ensure their retention for dictation, the copying and transcription of any words or phrases posing problems of spelling, punctuation or knowledge of English usage.

(vi) Corrections of work already done in class. This is a vital part of homework, but again, its value will depend very much on the thoroughness of checking and "follow-up."

QUESTION 6

How can homework be most effectively checked?

ANSWER 6

The effective checking of homework tends to impinge heavily on the teacher's time, but it should always be remembered that the majority of students learning shorthand are learning for vocational purposes in which they are expected to check back the correctness of their transcript. Checking is an important part of their work in after-life and students can assist in the quantitive checking of homework. Quality must be judged by the teacher, but students must be made to realize that although they assist in checking each other's work the quality is important. There should always be follow-up classroom work on faults which are disclosed in the checking of homework exercises. Ways of doing this are to check the work of student checkers regularly, taking in three or four books at a time. Clearly, the teacher must give attention to both the student's shorthand and to transcripts, yet it is impossible to check all the written work of students. A valuable compromise is to check one short section (five or six lines) of the work of every student, and to vary this by checking in detail all the work of four or five students only.

QUESTION 7

Would you prepare speed tests with the class before dictating?

ANSWER 7

As the question is worded (and it is a very common

one in this form) the answer is "no." A test is a means of measuring progress and real progress cannot be measured if the work has been prepared beforehand. What is really meant by inquirers is: should dictated matter be prepared before dictating? The answer is "yes." The speed room is not a place for constant testing, testing being incidental to the work of the class. The work of the speed room is to develop manual dexterity and to increase shorthand vocabulary. Shorthand vocabulary is not increased easily by "trial and error," and dictated matter unprepared must be more or less the subject of "trial and error." All new words, all words that from his experience the teacher knows will present difficulty to the class with which he is dealing, should be dealt with, analysed, written and drilled upon before the piece is finally dictated. Even in advanced speed work, the proportion of fully prepared material dictated should remain high. The more accurately the shorthand is written, the better the chance of reaching high speeds.

QUESTION 8

Should theory tests be dictated?

ANSWER 8

The chief aim of shorthand is the swift recording of the spoken word. The aim therefore should be to teach shorthand in the way in which it will ultimately be used. This means that the vehicle through which exercises are worked should be the spoken rather than the written word, and it logically follows that the testing of the theory should be by means of dictation. A theory test should embrace all aspects of the total skill and should incorporate the writing into shorthand of continuous matter from the spoken word, reading (in the form of the transcription of printed shorthand), penmanship, position-writing and vocalization.

QUESTION 9

At what stage of my teaching should I answer logically questioners who ask the reason for particular outlines? Is it sufficient to reply that the *reason* will appear as progress is made with the study?

ANSWER 9

At no stage in the teaching of shorthand is it sufficient to say that the reason for not adopting a certain policy or using a certain outline will appear later. Students should not be mystified and a logical answer to a question is always justified. Thus, if a student asked why the teacher will not accept as an example of a word containing two strokes a combination in which at a later stage the halving principle is used, he should be satisfied and not left in doubt.

QUESTION 10

Can you give any idea of the speed that should be attained at, say, the end of two evening-class sessions covering approximately 100 hours?

ANSWER 10

It is not possible to give any idea of the specific speed after any given number of hours' teaching as students vary so much in their ability to acquire manual dexterity and also in the pace at which they can learn. It is, however, reasonable to expect a speed of 70–90 words per minute on matter consisting of the normal vocabulary of the average members of the class. This presupposes that exercises have been dictated from the beginning.

QUESTION 11

Have you any suggestions for homogeneous grouping

of students in the ordinary evening institute, the students being recruited mainly from secondary modern schools?

ANSWER 11

See page 135.

QUESTION 12

What is the minimum standard to be aimed at for "occupational competency?"

ANSWER 12

The minimum standard to be aimed at by the student seeking employment should be 100–120 words per minute. If the candidate has a good educational background with a vocabulary such as would be possessed by the student having had a complete secondary education, 80–90 words per minute is often sufficient. The minimum is not recommended as the standard to be aimed at.

QUESTION 13

Do you advocate that, at the first lesson, time is well spent which is given to a survey of the whole system, as, for instance, that based on *An Hour with Pitman's Shorthand*?

ANSWER 13

Some such survey as indicated in the question is of great value. It is a sound principle of teaching that the pupil should know the problem proposed before he can solve it.

QUESTION 14

Is ability to use shorthand, say, up to 120–140 words per minute an indispensable equipment of the shorthand teacher?

ANSWER 14

It may not be an indispensable part of the equipment of the shorthand teacher to be able to write at 140 words a minute, but it is certainly desirable. Example is always better than precept, and the teacher's pen and notebook and blackboard demonstrations at speeds of 100–140 words a minute will do much to arouse the emulation of students. It is also important that the teacher should have had practical experience of writing at these speeds and passing examinations in order to understand fully the student's practical problems. Other things being equal, a teacher who has a good speed qualification will certainly be more efficient.

QUESTION 15

In assessing errors, to what degree should I insist on dictionary outline?

ANSWER 15

The dictionary outline is suggestive only. It is an outline proposed by experts, but any outline not contrary to a fundamental principle and one which the student will write again and read when written is acceptable. This question arises by reason of the wealth of shorthand material in the Pitman system of shorthand. The dictionary is therefore selective; it is not a textbook and if the student follows the principles he cannot be expected to guess which of two alternatives, apparently to him equally facile, should be selected. Nevertheless, having said so much, it is important that the teacher should always call attention to the correct dictionary outline. There is always a good reason why it is to be preferred.

QUESTION 16

Is it your view that dictation should consist always of connected matter?

ANSWER 16

Dictation of connected matter is much more natural

than that of isolated words. It cannot, however, be laid down dogmatically that dictation should always be connected matter. A mixture of material is good and a change in method of presentation is always effective. Following the principle that a practical subject should be taught as it will be used, in general, words in context is the form in which they will be used. (See page 123.)

If, for example, short forms are dictated singly at declared speeds, the need to write them unhesitatingly at these speeds is given a sharp focus in the student's mind, and more diligent learning and practice will result.

QUESTION 17

Do you think there is any advantage in encouraging students to write on the blackboard?

ANSWER 17

Very little, because—

1. The size of outline and the manner of writing is different from that required in the student's notebook.

2. The media, chalk and board, are different from those which the student will be called upon to use in practice.

3. The student's inexperience may lead to the writing of wrong outlines, which is bad for his fellows.

QUESTION 18

Do you advocate collective (class) reading as a method of familiarizing the whole class quickly with a piece of new shorthand matter?

ANSWER 18

Assuming careful supervision collective class reading as an occasional exercise is a good means of giving the whole class an idea of the content of new shorthand matter.

The danger, however, is that the weaklings lean on the more experienced.

Any methods that lead to quick, fluent reading without hesitation are worth pursuing. Far too much class time is wasted in slow, laborious effort to decipher outlines. The place for such preparatory work is in preparation out of class.

QUESTION 19

In attacking a page of unfamiliar printed shorthand, would you advocate giving a key to the student at the first onset, on the ground that time given to "puzzling out" outlines is wasted?

ANSWER 19

The reply to this question depends entirely upon the method of presentation. If the teacher is dealing with the functional method a key might be used. Under control and supervision the time given to "puzzling out" outlines, provided that by this is meant analysing the outlines, is not wasted. (See also the answer to Question 18.)

QUESTION 20

At what stage do you suggest that letters taken in the shorthand class should be transcribed on the typewriter?

ANSWER 20

As soon as the student is able to take down a simple letter he should transcribe it on the typewriter provided the student has a knowledge of the keyboard and has been instructed in the matter of display. There can be no doubt that it is a great advantage for the student to work on the typewriter, first from printed shorthand and afterwards from his own notes, as soon as he can.

QUESTION 21

Are there any real advantages as between pen and pencil for pupils in the early stages?

ANSWER 21

There is a real advantage as between pen and pencil for pupils in the early stages of shorthand learning. The pencil is not permanent, light and heavy distinctions are not always possible, the point may fail and the vowel insertion become indifferent, and experience suggests that the pencil lends itself to slackness and untidiness. On the other hand the pen point properly used is permanent, the differentiation between strokes is uniform and the writing is always legible. A good shorthand pen is always preferable to a good pencil.

QUESTION 22

In arranging a time-table for four hours a week, would you prefer one hour each day or two periods of two hours each?

ANSWER 22

One hour each day is the best arrangement as in all cases of skill learning regular daily periods of practice are superior to more widely spaced practices of longer duration.

QUESTION 23

I teach in a secondary (technical) school, which children enter at 11 + under an agreement to remain four years. How would you apportion the time for shorthand so that they could leave at 15 or 15 + with an average of 80–100 words per minute?

ANSWER 23

Shorthand could be taken in the last two years in

order to obtain the desired result. With five teaching periods (one each day) and 20–30 minutes' homework on three days in the week there should be no difficulty in reaching this level of attainment.

QUESTION 24

Teachers are urged to develop early a "sense of power." In this connexion is it your view that the first examination should be a *theory* examination, or an examination for taking dictation at, say, 50–60 words per minute?

ANSWER 24

It is suggested that classroom tests should take place before the first theory examination and that these and also the theory examination itself should be from dictation. They should consist of, at any rate in part, connected matter, giving the student the feeling that he is doing something which is of actual practical value. If dictation is used from the beginning the problem as stated never arises. (See also the answer to Question 8.)

QUESTION 25

In view of the growing popularity of the Intensive Course, what safeguards do you advocate to prevent its becoming a "snare"?

ANSWER 25

An Intensive Course as related to the teaching of shorthand may have one or two meanings. An Intensive Course in which some teaching and practice takes place on each of the six working days of the week is not a snare, but the attempt to cram the rules of Pitman's shorthand without devoting sufficient time to skill acquirement is certainly a snare.

QUESTION 26

At what stage in shorthand teaching would you qualify

the dictum: "Never dictate matter which will not be read back"?

ANSWER 26

When doing practical reporting, as at this stage the dictum is unnecessary. The shorthand is definitely written for the purpose of reading back.

QUESTION 27

What standards of attainment should be required for the short forms?

ANSWER 27

One needs to be uncompromising on this subject. The standards required should be demanded from the outset and insisted upon at every stage during instruction. Short form drills are often given in continuous sentence context and this method is certainly good. Absolute accuracy of shorthand writing and reading is necessary. When short forms are dictated singly in groups of twenty, thirty or forty, an initial standard of 50 words a minute should be required. Halfway through the theory the rate (timed by stopwatch) should be raised to 60 words a minute, and thereafter by stages advanced to 80 words a minute at the end of the theory, and thereafter.

QUESTION 28

How should one deal with the phrases? Should they be taught and drilled in the same way as the short forms?

ANSWER 28

The best short answer to this question is given in the Preface to *High-speed Shorthand Round the World*, a seventeen-page manifesto on the art of shorthand, which every teacher should read and re-read. Miss Emily D. Smith says: "Phrase writing is a wonderful servant but a bad master, and the wise course seems to be to phrase whenever it is useful to do so but not to seek ways of phrasing merely for the sake of phrasing."

Certainly there are some phrases which must become as indispensable a part of the good shorthand writer's equipment as the short forms themselves, (e.g. and the, we are, they were, it is, etc.). Therefore, drill on such phrases is necessary and important.

On the other hand, students may easily suffer from a momentary writing "block," if phrasing has been given too much emphasis. The important thing is that the principles of phrasing should be properly understood and applied effortlessly. The best way of achieving this is to work through *The New Phonographic Phrase Book*, a text which has a much wider value than the increase in phrasing facility alone.

QUESTION 29

What steps can be taken to correlate shorthand, typewriting, and English?

ANSWER 29

The importance of such correlation is generally recognized. A fundamental approach would be to group together all periods of teaching at present allocated as shorthand, typewriting, and English under the single title of Basic Office Skills and then to arrange the programme as a combined operation under the joint control of two or more teachers. In many schools such a scheme is impracticable.

Certainly teachers of shorthand should have a close liaison with teachers of typewriting and English. It would need a very long answer to develop in detail the ways in which this liaison could operate. Teachers will find considerable assistance in referring to the *Shorthand-typists' Transcription Course.*

QUESTION 30

What visual and audio aids are of most value to shorthand teachers?

ANSWER 30

The tape recorder, the dictation machine, the epigraph (overhead projector), the electronic stencil, and the slide projector (with variable exposure time).

Teachers should refer to the pamphlet on "Visual Aids" by L. S. Powell, published by the British Association for Commercial and Industrial Education.

CHAPTER XV

SYLLABUSES FOR COURSES IN SHORTHAND
(*a*) NEW COURSE (*b*) MODERN COURSE

THE schemes that follow could be used by teachers in all types of courses. The degree of intensity with which they are applied will naturally depend on the age and ability of the students and the time allowed for study and for out-of-class preparation and exercise work. It ought to be said, however, that for the acquisition of a time-skill like shorthand, intensive daily work with a generous allocation of time, both in class and out of it, will normally produce the best results. In this matter, students in full-time day classes are generally better served than evening students. Such students, however, could often be helped more than they are by having their work spread over at least two, and preferably more, evenings a week. One hour on each of four evenings is probably asking too much in these days even for very strongly motivated students. Nevertheless, three one-hour classes on three separate evenings are better than two two-hour periods on two evenings. In any case, the habit should be inculcated of requiring evening students to do some specific work every day. The value of it will soon become apparent to them. Fair-copying, reading preparation and drills on the short forms are the best kinds of work for students to do out of class.

The syllabuses are suggestive only. No teacher can say what difficulties may be encountered in the course of a lesson, nor, with any precision, what amount of ground it will be possible to cover. Similarly, the pattern of the lesson itself, how its constituent parts are to be dealt with, and what degree of emphasis is to be given to its various elements are all in the hands of the teacher.

Teachers of limited experience or those still seeking their skill teaching qualifications may find some suggestions of general application helpful, no matter what textbook or teaching methods are being used.

Suggestions to Teachers of Shorthand Theory

1. The foundation of good shorthand writing (and therefore good shorthand reading) is laid early in the course. Therefore some specific and separate attention is necessary to penmanship in every lesson.

2. The items to concentrate on in the teaching of penmanship are—

(*a*) lightness of stroke; nearly all students write far too heavily,

(*b*) size of stroke; students should be trained to write a style which will allow 15–20 words to be written in a line of the Shorthand Notebook, i.e. about 10–14 outlines,

(*c*) uniformity of size,

(*d*) technique of writing particular shorthand devices.

3. Encourage fast reading at all times. The teacher should read the shorthand to the students twice if necessary, the students should re-read it all together and then singly. In fact, all steps should be taken to ensure that the pace of reading is kept fast and alive from the start. Do not waste time spelling out the outlines or waiting for a student to struggle with an outline. It is true that this is a necessary intellectual discipline, but usually the place for it is out of class.

4. It is a mistake to ask students to read in a known or regular order. They are tempted to ignore everything except what they forecast as their own individual task.

5. Very little "free" dictation should be given during the theory stage—just enough to keep the students' interest alive and no more. Most of the work should be copying, copied-dictation (the dictation coming from the teacher or from selected students who may be relied on to keep a good pace), second copies at increasing speeds on lines left free for such copying (e.g. at 50, 60, and after about 10–15 weeks of shorthand at 70 and 80 words a minute).

6. Every theory class should be characterized by pace, effort and drive. This need not be continuous, of course, but there should be well defined peaks of effort with well defined goals to be aimed at. The class should never be at the point where twenty-four are idling and only one is really working.

7. Avoid too much concentration on separate words. In building the vocabulary of the students some attention must be given to separate words as new theory is introduced, but most of the development of vocabulary should arise from words in context. It is unnecessary to go through all the words given separately in order to establish a principle. This can be done at home, or by recapitulation during reading and copying.

8. The short forms should be given attention in every lesson without exception and the standard required for their writing and reading should be high from the start, viz. a dictation speed for single short forms of 60 words a minute. The short forms must become completely

automatic right from the start and *during the theory instruction*. No individual short form should be left undrilled for longer than two to three days in the early part of the theory or a week during the later stages. This will mean that it is necessary to drill at least twenty short forms in every lesson.

9. Much of the *consolidation* of theory learning should be done incidentally by question and answer while shorthand reading or copying is going on.

10. Never continue one activity to the point where students are bored with it. Vary the lesson by a variety of activities. In the first instance it is not necessary that the *whole* of an exercise should be copied to dictation at one time; half can be done in the early part of a lesson and half later. Similarly, vary as often as possible the methods of reading and writing called for from the students. Students should never be in the position of knowing exactly what is coming next.

11. Use (but do not over-use) rivalry and emulation as spurs to effort. Exhibit good work.

12. During the theory instruction almost the entire concentration should be on the shorthand. Longhand transcription should form the smallest possible fraction of the total time. A broad principle of theory will often help the student to grasp an idea and understand it, better than overmuch delving into detail. For example, the apparent rules for writing *r* other than the basic rule all spring from the general rule that under certain circumstances, the appropriate form of *r* is the form that is the easiest to write and to read (downward before *m*; upward before *t, d, ch, g, th, kl*; upward

after a straight upstroke; upward after two downstrokes, etc.).

13. Insist upon neat and orderly work from the start. Make the correct use of margins, date all work, give references, have a single line struck through all completed work no longer required, give the students brief opportunities of re-reading and improving their own notes exactly as an efficient shorthand-typist would.

14. Use progress charts and diagrams to maintain and stimulate the interest of the students.

15. Circulate among the students. There is much to be learnt from observation of what individuals are doing, and by talking to them. Opportunities for this occur during silent reading, copied-dictation, timed-copying, or sound-tape drills.

16. By the quick questioning of individuals make sure that the class knows and is *thinking about* what it is doing. It is easy for copying or even reading to become mindless and in these circumstances no true learning is taking place.

17. Work *with* the students and *among* the students all the time. Only on rare occasions may a shorthand class be left to carry on without direct guidance, and contact as a class. These are the occasions for individual tutorial work.

18. Let your own blackboard work be a model of fast, fluent writing. With small groups of students use the still better technique of demonstrating with pen and paper what you are aiming at.

19. Be careful to allocate your time correctly in every lesson. Remember that in every lesson there should be at least these elements: reading accurate shorthand; reading

own notes; question and answer on past points of theory; copying; copied-dictation; drill on short forms; specific attention to penmanship; expansion of vocabulary and theoretical knowledge.

Remember that reference should be made all the time to points of English as they arise.

20. The skill, knowledge, energy and enthusiasm of the teacher will foster corresponding qualities in the students.

21. A large part of the development of shorthand skill lies in the formation of correct habits. Therefore, checking becomes a most important part of teaching.

22. There are many indispensable phrases. These should be as automatic as the short forms. There are very many more which must be allowed to come naturally, and this can only happen if the *principle* underlying the phrase is thoroughly understood, e.g. "more than" is in the first category, "taller than," "finer than," in the second.

23. The linking up of new knowledge with what is already known is an essential teaching process.

24. When giving work to be done out of class, discuss it with the students. They must be perfectly clear about what is to be done, how it is to be done, and the target.

(a) New Course Syllabus

(i) The teaching syllabus is divided into: 11 teaching units for "A" section; 10 teaching units for "B" section; 12 teaching units for "C" section; 17 teaching units for "Theory" section; at the end of each section there is a grading test.

(ii) Revisionary periods of varying length are allowed for at the end of each Section of the two syllabuses.

(iii) Shorthand fountain-pens or dip pens must be used.

(iv) Students should be continuously encouraged to observe correct posture, the correct hold on the pen, and the correct techniques of shorthand writing.

(v) The *Student's Review* should be put to full use once the students have reached the early speed classes.

(vi) *Pitman's Office Training* should be used at "C" stage.

Chapters	I–VII	Section	"A"	Exercises	1–23
,,	VIII–X	,,	"B"	,,	24–60
,,	XI–XII	,,	"C"	,,	61–98
,,	XIII–XVIII	,,	"Theory"	,,	99–140

SECTION "A"

CHAPTERS I–VII: EXERCISES 1–23

Teaching Unit	*Chapter*	*Paragraphs*	*Exercises*	*Facility Drills*	*Graded Dictation Studies*	*Separate Word Groups*
					Pages:	
1	I	1–7	1	1–2	5	
2	II	8–9	2–3	3–4	6–7	
3	III	10	4–6	5–8	8–9	
4	IV	11–12	7–9	9–12	10–11	
5	V	13	10–12	13–14	12–14	1–2000 words
6	VI	14–15	13–14	15–16	12–14	2001–5000 ,,
7	VII	16	15–16	17–18	15–17	1–1000 ,,
8	VII	17	17–18	19	15–17	1001–3000 ,,
9	VII	18–19	19–21	20	15–17	3001–5000 ,,
10	VII	20	22–23	21–22	18–20	1–2000 ,,
11	Revision					

SECTION "B"

CHAPTERS VIII–X: EXERCISES 24–60

Teaching Unit	*Chapter*	*Paragraphs*	*Exercises*	*Facility Drills*	*Graded Dictation Studies*	*Separate Word groups*
					Pages:	
1	VIII	21–23	24–28	23–24	18–20	2001–5000 words
2	VIII	24–27	29–30	25–27	21–24	1–1000 ,,
3	IX	28–29	31–32	28–29	21–24	1001–3000 ,,
4	IX	30–31	33–35	30–32	21–24	3001–5000 ,,
5	IX	32	36–41	33–34	25–30	1–1000 ,,
6	X	33	42–43	35–36	25–30	1001–3000 ,,
7	X	34	44–48	37	25–30	3001–4000 ,,
8	X	35	49–54	38	25–30	4001–5000 ,,
9	X	36–37	55–60	39	31–38	1–5000 ,,
10	No Revision					

SECTION "C"

CHAPTERS XI–XII: EXERCISES 61–98

Teaching Unit	*Chapter*	*Paragraphs*	*Exercises*	*Facility Drills*	*Graded Dictation Studies*	*Separate Word groups*
					Pages	
1	XI	38	61–64	40	31–38	501–1000 words
2	XI	39	65–68	41	31–38	1001–2000 ,,
3	XI	40	69–70	42	31–38	2001–3000 ,,
4	XI	41	71–76	43	31–38	3001–4000 ,,
5	XI	42	77–79	44	31–38	4001–5000 ,,
6	XI	43–45	80–82	45–46	39–47	1–1000 ,,
7	XII	46	83–84	47–48	39–47	1001–2000 ,,
8	XII	47	85–86	49–50	39–47	2001–3000 ,,
9	XII	48	87–89	51–52	39–47	3001–4000 ,,
10	XII	49	90–92	53–54	39–47	4001–5000 ,,
11	XII	50–54	93–98	55–59	48–56	1–2000 ,,
12	Revision					

SECTION "THEORY"

CHAPTERS XIII–XVIII: EXERCISES 99–140

Teaching Unit	*Chapter*	*Paragraphs*	*Exercises*	*Facility Drills*	*Graded Dictation Studies*	*Separate Word groups*
					Pages:	
1	XIII	55–56	99–100	60–64	48–56	2001–5000 words
2	XIII	57–59	101–108	65	57–64	1–2000 ,,
3	XIV	60–61	109–112	66	57–64	2001–4000 ,,
4	XIV	62	113	Nil	57–64	4001–5000 ,,
5	XIV	63	114–116	67	65–72	1–1000 ,,
6	XV	64	117	68	65–72	2001–3000 ,,
7	XV	65–67	118–122	69	65–72	3001–4000 ,,
8	XV	68	123–124	70	65–72	4001–5000 ,,
9	XV	69–72	125–127	71–72	73–81	1–1000 ,,
10	XVI	73–74	128	73	73–81	1001–2000 ,,
11	XVI	75	129–130	74	73–81	2001–3000 ,,
12	XVI	76	Nil	75–76	73–81	3001–5000 ,,
13	XVI	77	131–134	77–82	82–90	1–5000 ,,
14	XVII	78–83	135–137	83–86	91–98	1–5000 ,,
15	XVIII	84–86	138–140	87–88	99–106	1–5000 ,,
16	Revision			89	99–106	2001–4000 ,,
17	Revision			90	99–106	4001–5000 ,,

A typical Section Test for elementary students is given below. When they take this test, students will have completed Chapter I–XII of the *New Course*.

Section Test "C"

Question 1. One hundred words in printed vocalized shorthand to be transcribed. Twenty minutes are allowed for the transcript.

It was a beautiful house, not too large for us, and it had a lovely garden with fruit trees and limes. The items of furnishing which were for sale were very suitable. There was a leather three-piece suite which looked quite new, two fireside chairs, an oak dining-table and four dining chairs, a very nice bureau, two divans, and of course, the curtains and fittings belonging to each room—they, too were gold. We decided to take it.

Questions 2 and 3. Two two-minute dictations at 30 w.p.m. The first is in the nature of a "warm-up," but students are credited with whichever of the passages they write the more accurately.

(*a*)

The main roads of this country are so full of traffic that
there is little pleasure in driving along them / and many of $\frac{1}{2}$
the other roads are in such a bad statc. If it is nccessary
for one to travel // from north to south and one wishes to **1**
view the countryside as one goes along it is better to make / $\frac{1}{2}$
a plan, taking a course along roads which are not used so
much. It is pleasing on a summer day. // **2**

(*b*)

I like to listen to the wireless but like to choose my programmes and not have it on all the time. / I think it is a very $\frac{1}{2}$
pleasant pastime on a dark and cold evening to sit round
the fire // and listen to a play or some good music or again if **1**
one wants to be amused a good variety / is very acceptable. $\frac{1}{2}$
I very rarely go to the cinema now because of programmes
I do not want to miss. // **2**

Question 4. Students are given longhand and shorthand outlines of ten words. These they have to copy in shorthand, positioning and vocalizing correctly.

autumn	robin
dances	lemons
lawns	flounces
mince	authors
prudence	glass

Question 5. Students are given a ten-word sentence written in cursive shorthand. They have to copy this for one minute as neatly and as quickly as they can.

(Six completely accurately written copies are expected.)

"We were unable to obtain a fair price for it."

(b) Modern Course Syllabus

The *Modern Course* is a very clear and practical presentation of the shorthand system. In combination with its two Exercise and Drill Notebooks it lends itself very well to either class instruction or individual learning. A mature student would find no difficulty in using the textbook and its notebooks as a "teach yourself" compendium. When students in a class using another textbook begin to lag behind the majority, the *Modern Course* is an excellent supplementary means of instruction.

Its organization is pedagogically sound. It sets out to teach the skill first through the eye, then through the eye and fingers in combination, and then through ear, fingers and eye together. Dictation practice material is provided from the very first lesson and, of course, dictation should form a part of every lesson. The presentation always begins without rules. One learns from the outset by deductive and functional processes. Once a reasonable familiarity with the new material has been built up by reading, copying, re-reading, re-copying, and then recording from dictation, the rules are developed in a Summary.

Here the teacher will clearly not use the letterpress, admirably as it is compiled. It will be better to make this presentation of rule by short oral explanation followed by illustration, question and answer, and recapitulation. Since the summaries commonly contain a fair amount of material requiring intellectual application, the work should be broken up with copying from the blackboard and reading back from the notes made. This will be necessary before the student is ready to go on to the Exercise based on the Summary, and given in the Exercise and Drill Notebook.

The short forms should be taught (that is to say, they should be explained and the reasons for their manner of representation clearly understood). They should also be drilled on the cyclic plan previously described.

The longhand section of the Exercise based on the Summary may conveniently be used from time to time as a check on the theoretical knowledge and accuracy. The longhand exercises other than this however, should be dictated first, after thorough work on the preceding shorthand exercises. That is to say, they should be dictated before the student reads them through or attempts to write from the longhand. It may be necessary sometimes with less able students to prepare the longhand exercise by dealing with any known or revealed weaknesses by blackboard work and copying into an ordinary notebook before the dictation begins.

Some of the copying of shorthand may be done silently at the student's own pace. Some should certainly be done at a controlled pace, either at the dictation of the teacher, or at the dictation and simultaneous copying of the better students. Such work helps to build and strengthen the link between voice, ear (aural comprehension), and motor response and skill.

During the work that precedes the Summary it will be found that the *Modern Course* is very conveniently arranged so that the edge of a sheet of paper or of a notebook may be laid along the longhand column covering it and leaving the columns of shorthand examples to be re-read from the shorthand.

Obviously, teachers will vary their methods both to

bring variety into class work, and to cater for the differences in age and ability of various groups of students. Enough has been said, however, to give teachers a sound basis of approach to teaching the skill through the *Modern Course*.

The Exercise and Drill Notebooks give a most necessary emphasis to good penmanship and lend themselves to facility work which should form a regular part of every lesson. Here it is essential that the teacher devote some time during every lesson concentrating on the penmanship skill of a few different individuals in each lesson. Such attention should be given primarily as help, guidance and suggestion in a positive way, rather than criticism and fault-finding in a negative way.

Assuming that out-of-class work is to form part of the course, then the *Modern Course* provides ample material for a variety of valuable and skill-building exercises. Some examples are now given—

(i) Prepare an exercise for rapid reading and make one shorthand copy of it on the first line provided.

(ii) Study one of the summaries (or part of a summary), copy the examples given a specified number of times, and prepare to apply the knowledge gained to the writing of other similar examples in class.

(iii) Copy and learn ready for dictation at 40–80 words a minute (according to the stage of study reached) two or three specified groups of short forms.

(iv) By reading and copying two or three times, prepare exercise for free dictation in an ordinary notebook.

(v) Copy two or three groups of phrases and prepare them for dictation in simple sentences.

(vi) Prepare two or three lines for fast, controlled penmanship so that they may be written accurately from dictation at speeds of 50–100 words a minute (according to the stage of study reached).

(vii) (As occasional exercises only.) Write a few lines specified from the longhand into shorthand.

Write a list of words issued in typescript to the students from the rules given in a particular Summary (or part of a Summary).

The table on the following pages presents an arrangement of The *Modern Course* in forty-five units of work with Review Tests spaced at convenient points in the syllabus.

Scheme of Lessons Based on the "Modern Course"

The following is a suggested syllabus covering 48 one-hour lessons, which may be divided into weeks, with one hour allowed for homework for each two hours of instruction. Dictation practice should form part of every class lesson. At the end of the course students should have a knowledge of the whole of the theory, and should have acquired a writing speed of 60 words per minute, or more, according to ability.

Lessons covering the first four hours only are given in detail.

FIRST HOUR

Chapter One

Write on the blackboard the outlines for *pay*, *paid*, *page*, *day*, *date*, *up*, *touch*, *judge*. Explain how the outlines are built up, and stress the fact that shorthand outlines are

Teaching Unit	*Chapter Section and Pages*	*Exercises*	*S.F's*	*Content*
1	Ch. 1, §1–3, pp. 7–10	1, 2	pp. 9 and 10	*p*, *b*, *t*, *d*, *Ch*, *j*. Two vowels
2	Ch. 1, § 4 and Summary, pp. 10–13	3, 4	pp. 9 and 10	*ay* and *u*
3	Ch. 2, § 5, pp. 14–15	5, 6	p. 15	*k*, *g*, *m*, *n*, *ng*. Two vowels
4	Ch. 2, § 6 and Summary, pp. 16–17	7, 8	pp. 9, 10 and 15	*e* and *oh*
5	Ch. 3, § 7, 8, pp. 18, 19	9, 10	pp. 18, 19	Circle *s*
6	Ch. 3, Summary and Table, pp. 20, 21	11, 12	p. 21	Circle *s*
7	Ch. 4, § 9, pp. 22, 23	13, 14	p. 23	More Consonants
8	Ch. 4, Summary, p. 24	15, 16	p. 21	Circle and Stroke
9	Ch. 5, § 10 and Summary, pp. 26–29	17–20	p. 27 and p. 23	First-place vowels
10	Ch. 6, § 11–13 and Summary, pp. 30–32	21–24	p. 31 and p. 33	Third-place vowels
11	Ch. 7, § 14–15 and Summary, pp. 34–37	25–28	p. 35 and p. 33	*l* and Diphthong '*i*'
12	Ch. 8, § 16 and Summary, pp. 38–39	29–32	pp. 38, 39 and p. 21	*w* and *y*; Diphthong '*oi*'
13	Ch. 9, § 18, 19 and Summary, pp. 40–43	33–36	p. 41 and p. 21	*r* Up and Down: Diph. '*ow*'
14	Ch. 10, § 20, 21 and Summary, pp. 44–47	37–40	p. 45 and p. 33	*h* Up and Down and Tick. Diph. '*u*'
15	Ch. 11, § 22–24	41, 42	p. 21	Review of consonants, vowels and diphthongs
16	Review			
17	Ch. 12, § 25 and Summary, pp. 50–52	43–46	p. 51 and p. 33	*sway* and *sez* Circles
18	Ch. 13, § 26, 27 and Summary, pp. 53—55	47–50	p. 54 and p. 21	*st*, *ster*, *con*.
19	Ch. 14, § 28 and Summary, pp. 57–59	51–54	p. 58 and p. 33	Halving for *t*
20	Ch. 15, § 29 and Summary, pp. 60–62	55–58	pp. 60, 58, 54	Halving for *d*
21	Ch. 16, § 30 and Summary, pp. 62–63	59–62	pp. 62, 51, 45	Doubling
22	Ch. 17, § 31, pp. 64–66	63, 64	pp. 65, 41, 38, 39	*r* hook to straight strokes. Dot *h*

23	Ch. 17, Summary, pp. 64–66	65–66	pp. 65, 35, 21	*r* hook to Straight Strokes. Dot *h*
24	Ch. 18, § 32 and Summary, pp. 67–68	67–70	pp. 67, 51, 45	*l* hook to Straight Strokes
25	Ch. 19, § 33 and Summary, pp. 69–71	71–74	pp, 70, 62, 60	*n* hook to Straight Strokes
26	Ch. 20, § 34 and Summary, pp. 72–73	75–78	pp. 72, 59, 54	*f* and *r* hook to Straight Strokes
27	Ch. 21, § 35–36, pp. 74–75	79, 80	pp. 75, 21	*r* and *l* Hook to curves
28	Ch. 21, Summary, pp. 75–77	81, 82	pp. 75, 33	*r* and *l* Hook to curves
29	Ch. 22, § 37 and Summary, pp. 78, 79	83–86	pp. 78, 38, 39, 41	*n* hook to curves
30	Ch. 23, § 38, pp. 80, 81	87, 88	pp. 80, 81, 45	*shun* hook
31	Ch. 23, Summary, pp. 81, 82	89, 90	pp. 80, 81, 51, 54	*shun* hook
32	Ch. 24, § 40 and Summary, pp. 83–84	91–94	pp. 83, 58, 60, 62	Circle *s* to hooks
33	Ch. 25, § 41 and Summary, pp. 85, 87	95–98	pp. 85, 65, 67, 70	Circles, loops and hooks combined
34	Review		pp. 21 and 33	
35	Ch. 26, § 42 and Summary, pp. 88–90	99–102	pp. 88, 72, 75, 78	Compound Consonants
36	Ch. 27, § 43 and Summary pp. 91–92	103–106	pp. 91, 80, 83, 85	Abbreviated *w*
37	Ch. 28, § 44 and Summary, pp. 92–93	107–110	pp. 93, 35, 41, 45	Diphones
38	Ch. 29, § 45, pp. 94, 95	111–112	pp. 95, 51, 54, 58	Prefixes and Suffixes
39	Ch. 29, Summary, pp. 96–98	113–114	pp. 95, 60, 62, 65	Prefixes and Suffixes
40	Ch. 30, § 46 and Summary, pp. 99–101	115–118	pp. 99, 67, 70, 72	Intersections
41	Ch. 31, Summary, Part I, pp. 101–108	119	pp. 21, 33	Vowels and Vowel Indication
42	Ch. 31, Summary, Part II, pp. 109–114	120	pp. 75, 78, 80	Vowels and Vowel Indication
43	Ch. 31, Part II, pp. 115–121	121, 122	pp. 83, 85, 88, 91	Abbreviating Devices
44	Ch. 32, pp. 122–130	123, 125	pp. 93, 95, 99	Reading, Copying, Dictating
45	Review			

§ Section Ch. Chapter

based on *sound*, not on longhand spelling. Point out that in the words under consideration: (i) the long vowel-sound *ae* is represented in longhand by the combinations *ay*, *ai* and *a/e*; (ii) the consonant-sound *j* by *g*, *j* and *dg*; and (iii) the short vowel-sound *ŭ* by *u*, *ou* and *u/e*. In Pitman's shorthand there is one sign only to represent such sounds.

Stress the fact that the first downstroke of the outline rests on the line, and dictate these eight words several times, reaching a dictation speed of 24 words per minute.

Demonstrate the use of the six straight downstrokes and the use of the vowel-signs for *ae* and *ŭ* before and after strokes. Teach the grammalogue signs for *a*, *the*, *of*, *to*, *be*, *it*, and dictate slowly such word-groups as: *the page; the date; to pay it; a page of it;* etc.

SECOND HOUR

Chapter One (*Contd.*)

Re-dictate the word-groups already practised. Teach remainder of grammalogues and contractions shown on pages 9 and 10, dictating the words several times. Demonstrate the use of *tick the*. Practise, by blackboard demonstration and class dictation, the phrases given on page 10.

The students should at this point be able easily to read aloud the sentences given in Exercise 1 of the *Drill Notebook*. Dictate Exercise 3. Exercise 2 should be read through, and then carefully but freely copied by the students, while the teacher passes from student to student, looking at the attempt made with Exercise 3.

Homework

Chapter One should be read in detail, taking particular note of the instructions on the writing of shorthand given on pages 10–12. After the rules given in the Summary on pages 12–13 have been studied, Exercise 4 should be worked. Students must be trained to apply their knowledge. If they can write *pay* they should experience no difficulty in writing *bay*, and so on.

THIRD HOUR

Chapter Two

Students are now familiar with the idea of writing from dictation, and Exercise 3 should be re-dictated. Exercise 4 should also be dictated after dealing with any points of difficulty which the students may have experienced in working this exercise.

Illustrate on the blackboard those words from page 14 which use the strokes for *Kay Gay*, *eM*, *eN iNG*, but which use only the known vowel-signs *ae* and *ŭ*. Dictate these outlines several times. Place on the blackboard outlines using the vowel-signs for *ĕ* and *oe*, and demonstrate the pairing of the vowel-signs for *ae* and *ĕ*; *oe* and *ŭ*.

Teach and dictate the grammalogues and contractions given on page 15.

Dictate simple word-groups using these new signs, as: *you take it; that is his cheque; I paid you; change the cheque*, etc. Students should reach speeds of 30–40 words per minute on such very simple matter by means of repetition.

FOURTH HOUR

Chapter Two (*Contd.*)

The phrases given on page 15 should be studied and then written from dictation. The teacher must insist from the outset upon a light and neat style of writing.

Exercise 5 should be used for class reading and afterwards dictated. Exercise 7 should be dictated.

Homework

After a study of Chapter Two, with particular regard to the Summary given on pages 16 and 17, students should work Exercise 8. When setting this homework the teacher should again stress the application of rules from one word to another. If the outline for *take* is known there should be no difficulty in writing *tuck* correctly; if the outline for *get* is familiar that for *gate* should cause no difficulty.

Students should be encouraged to use Exercise 6 as a "facility" exercise, first reading the sentences and then copying the shorthand over and over again, writing lightly and quickly, and returning quickly from the end of one line to the beginning of the next.

General Note

The remainder of this syllabus is not given in detail as the teacher will be able to adapt the details of his teaching to the particular requirements of his class. It is emphasized again, however, that the lists of outlines given with each chapter should be dictated and re-dictated, so that the students acquire a good writing speed and are able to represent without hesitation the shorthand forms for those words which are the most common in the English language.

In all future lessons, also, full use should be made of the *Exercise and Drill Notebook*, using it to give practice in the reading of accurate shorthand, for dictation purposes, for facility practice, and for tests of the students' knowledge of the rules. The final exercise given with each chapter should always be dictated on an occasion subsequent to the students working it.

FIFTH AND SIXTH HOURS

Chapter Three

Take advantage of the opportunity for word-building which this chapter presents. Give short talk on the value of vowel omission, pointing out the advantages which accrue to the speed writer from the wise omission of vowel-signs.

SEVENTH AND EIGHTH HOURS

Chapter Four

Draw the students' attention to the alternative signs for the very common sounds of *s* and *z*, and stress the principle that where there is an initial or final vowel there must be a stroke consonant against which to write the sign. This is a fundamental principle and should be thoroughly understood by students. Set a simple theory test, covering Chapters One to Four, and dictate a passage of, say, two minutes' duration at a speed of 30 words per minute.

NINTH AND TENTH HOURS

Chapter Five

Emphasize the fact that it is the position of the first vowel-sign in an outline which determines the position of that outline. Dictate pairs of illustrative words, such as *got*, *get;* *tax*, *takes;* *or*, *air*, etc. Reiterate the value of vowel omission, giving examples of its use, such as the outlines for the words *fact* and *effect*.

ELEVENTH AND TWELFTH HOURS

Chapter Six

Two points of interest are: (i) position of the third-place vowel when occurring between two consonant strokes; and (ii) the fact that there is no third position for outlines made up of horizontal strokes only. Test the students' knowledge of the grammalogues and contractions, using the table given on page 33.

THIRTEENTH AND FOURTEENTH HOURS

Chapter Seven

The value of vowel indication should again be mentioned, in order that the students may fully appreciate: (i) the rule allowing for the alternative directions in the writing of consonant *l*; and (ii) the value of the use of stroke *s* following a triphone, etc.

FIFTEENTH HOUR

Chapter Eight

SIXTEENTH AND SEVENTEENTH HOURS

Chapter Nine

Point out the further application of the principle of vowel indication, linking *r* with *l*. Dictate plenty of contrasting pairs of outlines, such as *car*, *carry*, etc.

EIGHTEENTH AND NINETEENTH HOURS

Chapter Ten

Point out that the *tick h* is written in the same direction as the downward form of *Hay*. *Tick h* should never take the slant of the grammalogue for *to*.

TWENTIETH HOUR

Chapter Eleven

Review the signs and the principles so far learnt, using the Table of Consonants given on page 48 and the summary of the vowel- and diphthong-signs given on page 49. Simple theory test, including tests on the grammalogues, contractions and phrases, and a dictation test of two and a half minutes' duration. The students should be able to reach a speed of 35–40 words per minute on simple matter.

TWENTY-FIRST HOUR

Chapter Twelve

Use word-building exercises to link the large circles with the small. Emphasize necessity for absolute distinction in size between the two circles, a slight exaggeration of size of the large circle being permissible. Appropriate phrases should be thoroughly practised, as they have a wide application in notetaking.

TWENTY-SECOND AND TWENTY-THIRD HOURS

Chapter Thirteen

Link up the loops with the circles by means of word-building exercises. Point out the high frequency of occurrence of the syllable *con*, *com*, *cog*, and watch students' subsequent notetaking to check up on the full use of the *con* dot and the writing of *con* by proximity. Students should study carefully the comparative table given on page 56.

TWENTY-FOURTH AND TWENTY-FIFTH HOURS

Chapter Fourteen

Interest the students in the ingenuity of the device of adding by halving. Point out non-use of the principle in the outlines for such words as *effect*, *minute*, etc., and, by adequate dictation, ensure that the students know how to use the halving principle in phrase writing.

TWENTY-SIXTH HOUR

Chapter Fifteen

Points to emphasize in this lesson are: (i) the treatment of the final syllable *-ed*; and (ii) the contrasting outlines in such words as *field* and *followed*; *hard* and *hurried.*

TWENTY-SEVENTH AND TWENTY-EIGHTH HOURS

Chapter Sixteen

Take the opportunity afforded by the double-length outlines to develop in students the habit of "flicking" long strokes quickly rather than laboriously drawing them. The quick "flick" should produce a tapering stroke. Theory test, including tests on the grammalogues and contractions, and a three-minute dictation passage at 40 words per minute.

TWENTY-NINTH AND THIRTIETH HOURS

Chapter Seventeen

Interest students in the fact that by means of the hook one simple sign is used to represent very common combinations of sounds.

THIRTY-FIRST HOUR

Chapter Eighteen

Link this chapter with the preceding one, and help the students to memorize the hooks by pointing out that the *l* hook is written with the *l*eft motion and the *r* hook with the *r*ight motion.

THIRTY-SECOND AND THIRTY-THIRD HOURS

Chapter Nineteen

Emphasize the fact that the use of a simple hook, combined with the application of the halving and doubling principles, enables the writer to represent some very common combinations of sound, such as *nt*, *nd*, *ntr*, etc., without additional manual effort. Phrases should be particularly noted.

THIRTY-FOURTH HOUR

Chapter Twenty

Link the teaching of the *f/v* hook with the *n* hook covered in preceding chapter. Phrases should again be particularly practised.

THIRTY-FIFTH AND THIRTY-SIXTH HOURS

Chapter Twenty-one

As with the small and large circles, so with the small and large hooks to curves—the distinction should be quite clear and slight exaggeration of the large hook is permissible.

THIRTY-SEVENTH HOUR

Chapter Twenty-two

Two points of interest are: (i) that the final hook must not be used when there is a following vowel (linking this up with the circles and loops); and (ii) that there is no final hook for *f/v* to curves.

THIRTY-EIGHTH HOUR

Chapter Twenty-three

Again, interest the students in the fact that the *shun* hook is yet another device for representing in one short sign a very common combination of sounds. Short test for theory, grammalogues, contractions and phrases, and a dictated passage of three minutes' duration at 50 words per minute.

THIRTY-NINTH HOUR

Chapter Twenty-four

Students must be trained to form the circle and the hook so that both are clearly shown, even when writing very quickly.

FORTIETH AND FORTY-FIRST HOURS

Chapter Twenty-five

Give careful instruction in the use of the small and large circles and loops combined with initial and final hooks, and devote time to a careful study of the comparative table given on page 87.

FORTY-SECOND HOUR

Chapter Twenty-six

When writing the exercises students should be asked to distinguish clearly between the large hook of *kw* and small hook of *kl*, and the large hook of *whl* and the small hook of *wl*.

The thickening of downward *r* and *l* should be done by a quick "flick" of the pen, the stroke tapering towards the end. Heavy writing of such strokes is a deterrent to speed.

FORTY-THIRD HOUR

CHAPTER TWENTY-SEVEN

Students should be trained to use the special signs for figures with rapidity, ease and accuracy. Much time is often wasted by inexperienced writers who laboriously write, for instance, six *o*'s when representing "one million."

FORTY-FOURTH HOUR

CHAPTER TWENTY-EIGHT

Students should understand the use of the diphones, but in actual shorthand writing the signs are rarely inserted.

FORTY-FIFTH HOUR

CHAPTER TWENTY-NINE

Students should memorize, by copying and writing from dictation, the signs for the common prefixes and suffixcs, as these forms are valuable time-savers in notetaking.

FORTY-SIXTH HOUR

CHAPTER THIRTY

The intersected signs should also be thoroughly memorized, as not only are "intersections" time-savers but they have the advantage that intersected phrases are extremely distinctive and legible.

FORTY-SEVENTH AND FORTY-EIGHTH HOURS

Chapter Thirty-one

Part One of this chapter summarizes knowledge already gained by students regarding use of vowel-signs, vowel indication and vowel omission. The Table of Special Outlines given on page 113 should be studied and memorized. The great majority of the grammalogues and contractions listed on pages 115–9 are already known to students.

Pages 120–1 of Chapter Thirty-one suggest further time-saving devices in which students will be interested. The phrases and outlines shown can be memorized by copying and writing from dictation.

Chapters Thirty-two and Thirty-three consist entirely of shorthand reading material, which, after having reached Chapter Twenty-nine, the students can read page by page, either in class or for homework. Test covering all the theory and including tests on the grammalogues and contractions. Speed test of three minutes' duration at 60 words per minute.

The foregoing schemes are not intended to be more than suggestive. They are intended to convey to the reader that something akin to the project plan can be designed by the teacher, and, although the student would not necessarily understand the assignment, he will be in a position to grasp the idea that he is intended to reach a certain point by a certain time. The possibility of being able to write continuous matter in shorthand will appeal to him, and the law of preparation or preparedness will immediately come into operation. The exercises that have been proposed in the foregoing schemes consist mainly of common words. No word that is not in general use has been included: indeed, 90 per cent of general business conversation and correspondence, apart from the technicalities of a particular business, consists of common words, and, consequently, in the course of theory lessons, common words only need to be introduced. Words occasionally met with should be the subject-matter of the revision lessons in the speed classes where the process of vocabulary building takes place. The student of theory, whilst building an ordinary vocabulary, has little time at his disposal for special rules or special words.

QUESTIONS

The following series of questions is intended to provide material for a revision of the subject-matter of this little volume.

CHAPTER I

1. What place does reading, writing and arithmetic take in a scheme of education?
2. Explain the expression: "reading, writing and arithmetic are the tools for handling experience."
3. What is the place of shorthand in a scheme of commercial education?
4. Explain what is meant by saying that shorthand is not an end in itself, rather a means to an end.
5. Explain what is meant by formal studies.
6. Rebut the criticism that shorthand, being strictly vocational, has no educational value.
7. "The subject-matter of teaching cannot be divorced from methods." Discuss this statement.
8. What is educational theory? Do you consider it to be stationary or progressive?
9. To what extent is a knowledge of psychology an essential part of a teacher's equipment?

CHAPTER II

1. In office life, a worker is called upon to exercise two kinds of mental activities. Describe these.
2. What is meant by the automatic activities in life?
3. What do you mean by stimulus-response bonds?
4. Justify the use of repetition matter in shorthand speed practice.
5. Explain: "practice makes perfect." Under what conditions is this untrue? What is needed to make it true of the time-skills?
6. What are the three laws at the root of educational practice?
7. What do you understand by consciousness?
8. Explain "field of consciousness," "focus," and "margin of consciousness."
9. What is the relationship between consciousness and attention, and between attention and interest?

10. Every impression is said to have its resultant expression. Explain this.
11. What is meant by "the law of effect"?

CHAPTER III

1. Define attention.
2. Distinguish between attention and interest in its fullest sense.
3. When may a matter be said to be interesting?
4. From whence does interest arise?
5. What advantage has shorthand over non-vocational subjects when considered in relation to what is known as "the law of readiness"?
6. Show how interest can be maintained in a formal subject like shorthand.
7. What is meant by "association"?
8. Show how association, interest and attention are related.
9. What is meant by saying that ideas are linked together in the mind in groups and that one idea may be found in several groups? Show how this view can be utilized in the teaching of shorthand theory.
10. What do you mean by "the law of preparation"?
11. Illustrate the law of preparation from the teaching of some principle in shorthand.
12. Of what value are mnemonics?
13. Explain how uninteresting things may be made to acquire an interest.
14. How would you prevent interest from waning?

CHAPTER IV

1. What do you mean by "ambition impulses"?
2. How can a teacher justifiably appeal to the instinct of self-esteem in a pupil?
3. Show how the teacher of shorthand can utilize the primary instinct of imitation.
4. Explain why you would or would not agree with Rousseau that "emulation is not an instinct to be appealed to."
5. Set out a convenient method for the writing of longhand into shorthand, making provision for re-writing and correction.
6. Is the use of sarcasm or irony ever justified in teaching?
7. Why is a teacher justified in appealing to the instinct of curiosity in his teaching?
8. What importance do you attach to the reading as distinct from the writing of shorthand?

9. Explain, with illustrations, what you mean by: "it is the new in the old that attracts attention."
10. Motive is said to be the root of interest. Explain this.
11. Define apperception and distinguish an appercept from a percept and a concept.
12. All persons do not apperceive a new object in the same way. Explain this.
13. Before framing a general rule what information would you require?

CHAPTER V

1. What do you mean by "the law of use"?
2. Justify the aim of the teacher who desires to form habits.
3. When do you consider that habitual action becomes dangerous?
4. Why should an attempt be made to make writing, spelling and shorthand writing automatic?
5. Explain what you mean by a reflex action.
6. Habit is said to be second nature. Justify this.
7. Are shorthand outlines written at speed written according to rule? Justify your view.
8. What is the general cause of the dwindling of numbers in evening classes? How would you seek to prevent this?
9. Explain what you mean by saying that shorthand is a matter of sensory motor co-ordination.
10. Justify the instruction that "a speed student should get down something of everything he hears."
11. Account for a mental hesitation in the case of a speed student who hears a word for the first time.

CHAPTER VI

1. What is a skill? What new factors are introduced in time-skills?
2. The complete learning of shorthand comprises the acquisition of three skills. Explain this.
3. What is the medium through which the skill of shorthand is learned?
4. For what purpose is the skill of the eye required in shorthand learning?
5. What is the advantage of learning to type shorthand transcripts?
6. In what respect does a skill subject differ from general subjects like history or geography in the curriculum?
7. Is there any advantage in the shorthand teacher being an expert in writing on the blackboard?

8. Explain what is meant by saying that an expert craftsman exercises his calling with ease, precision, smoothness and rhythm.
9. To what extent is the "telling method" useful in instructing a class engaged on a skill subject?
10. Explain why you would not draw a shorthand outline.

CHAPTER VII

1. What do you mean by memory?
2. What is the relationship between memory and habit?
3. What is meant by "native retentivity"?
4. To what extent can memory be improved by training?
5. What are the chief bases of recall?
6. Justify, or otherwise, the statement that first impressions are lasting.
7. What element is the most important in aiding memory?
8. What is a mnemonic, and can the use of such a device be justified?
9. Give three suitable mnemonics for use in shorthand teaching.
10. How does thinking aid memory?
11. What is your view of an Intensive Course of shorthand training?
12. Why is a university graduate not likely to have the necessary ability to learn shorthand more rapidly than any other student of average intelligence and fair general education?
13. What is your view on cramming, and can this device be utilized in the learning of shorthand?

CHAPTER VIII

1. Would you teach all you know of the halving principle before passing on to the double length?
2. What is meant by teaching on a simple vocabulary? What are the advantages and disadvantages of such a course?
3. The words used as examples in the *Instructor* are often beyond the scope of the vocabulary of an elementary class. Has this any effect on shorthand teaching?
4. What is meant by teaching on a common-word basis and where is the material to be found for such teaching?
5. Does teaching on a simplified vocabulary necessarily mean that the students' knowledge of theory is deficient?
6. What steps must be taken in the later stages of teaching to avoid an indifferent knowledge of the theory of shorthand where the approach has been through a common-word vocabulary?

CHAPTER IX

1. What do you mean by word frequency?
2. How is the so-called 700 Common Word List made up?
3. Can you explain why such a word as "saucer" is not in the list?
4. In the selection of the 700 Common Words what considerations other than frequency have been taken into account?
5. What derivatives of the 700 Common Words can reasonably be included in the selected vocabulary?
6. What do you mean by writing by rote, and how does a selected vocabulary help this form of shorthand writing?
7. In what way has the value of this particular word list been proved?
8. What is the relationship between teaching in a selected vocabulary and the statement that in teaching shorthand, dictation should commence at the beginning and theory continue to the end?
9. Write a note on the Dewey List of Word Frequency.

CHAPTER X

1. What do you mean by method in teaching?
2. State the various methods used in the classroom.
3. Explain the illustrative method and show how it can be used in the teaching of commercial subjects.
4. Illustrate the method of induction.
5. Is the inductive method a rapid method of teaching or a slow one? Give reasons.
6. What do you mean by deduction?
7. Describe the "telling" method and the "textbook" method.
8. How far is the lecture useful in shorthand teaching?
9. Suggest some methods for learning rules in shorthand.
10. How does imagination play a part in teaching?
11. What is the function of the question in class teaching?
12. Explain individual teaching and group teaching.
13. What is discipline? How is it (*a*) enforced, (*b*) developed, in class practice?

CHAPTER XI

1. Suggest a method of writing corrections without danger of style deteriorating.
2. If you were called upon to comment on the time to be devoted to shorthand practice, which would you suggest was the better, six hours' work each week-end, or one hour daily for five days in the week? Give reasons.

3. Why would you advise systematic revision of theory throughout a shorthand speed course?
4. Give lesson notes for an hour's work in the slow-speed room.
5. What is your view as to the duration of readings in speed practice?
6. Why is a teacher not justified in reading for speed practice without afterwards requiring a transcript or the reading of the shorthand note?
7. What is your view of repetition work in the speed room?
8. Justify the instruction: "correct errors in the speed room before they are made."
9. What do you mean by fair-copying? State the advantages to be obtained from this class of work.
10. State briefly how vocabulary commences and grows.
11. Some students adopt the small geometrical style and some the flowing cursive style for shorthand speed writing. Give your views on this matter.
12. What is your opinion on the size, dimensions and general characteristics of a notebook suitable for speed writing?
13. Give your views on reading from printed shorthand and from shorthand notes as a means of improving general shorthand knowledge.

INDEX